AWAKEN YOUR
AUTHENTIC LEADERSHIP

Lisa,
Looking forward to
co-creating a global
community of
authentic leaders

Ja

"A new era of awakened authentic leadership is emerging. Tana Heminsley's insightful and practical book provides a roadmap for those who are waking up to the call."

Dr Mark Atkinson, Physician & CEO of the Academy of Human Potential

"This book is an invitation to wake-up the leadership that lives in each of us: integrity, truth, alignment, and vision and takes us on a journey of how to make our way into clarity of our role. It is personal and professional and dynamic; an important resource for everyone who feels the quickening of their responsibility as a leader."

Heidi Mack M. Ed; PhD (c) Psychotherapist using authenticity – based interventions for wellness. Kingston Ontario

"Authentic Leadership is a concept whose time has come. Tana Heminsley has successfully built a bridge between the spiritual concepts of consciousness and awakening with the practical implications for leaders. This book serves as a step by step tool kit for any leader who is interested in living an authentic life."

Alison van Buuren, Executive Coach

"There is immense power and truthfulness coming through Tana Heminsley's words. This is a wonderful guide for the development of new ways of leading that begin in the heart and honor the wisdom we each inherit. Tana is helping to pave the path for a new wave of leaders with compassion, authenticity and many gems of wisdom."

Bettina Rothe, Somatic Leadership Coach & Founder of Soulful Steps

"It has often seemed to me, as a psychologist and coach, that most people are either running away from finding their true selves, or running towards finding a greater understanding of themselves and the people around them. This book provides a route map to finding your true, authentic self and is essential reading for anyone who has ever thought, "There must be more to life than this"."

Fiona Beddoes-Jones, CEO, The Cognitive Fitness Consultancy and Author of the *Authentic Leadership 360*

AWAKEN
YOUR
AUTHENTIC
LEADERSHIP

Lead with Inner Clarity and Purpose

TANA HEMINSLEY

AUTHENTIC LEADERSHIP GLOBAL
PUBLISHING DIVISION

Authentic Leadership Global, Inc. – Publishing Division
#303-628 Kinghorne Mews,
Vancouver, B.C.
Canada
V6Z 3H6
tana@leadauthentic.com
www.leadauthentic.com

Library and Archives Canada Cataloguing in Publication

Heminsley, Tana, 1962-, author
    Awaken your authentic leadership : lead with inner
clarity and purpose / Tana Heminsley ; foreward by Mike
Desjardins, Driver (CEO), ViRTUS.

Includes bibliographical references.
Issued in print and electronic formats.
ISBN 978-0-9918481-0-2 (pbk.).--ISBN 978-0-9918481-1-9 (eBook)

    1. Leadership. I. Title.

BF637.L4H45 2013   158'.4   C2013-903019-0
                                      C2013-903020-4

For my husband Chris—
for believing in me and supporting me—
I am grateful in so many ways!

ACKNOWLEDGEMENTS

This book is possible because of the support and influences of many people—my family and friends, the ViRTUS Inc. family who constantly inspire me to be better at what I do as well as a better person, the Authentic Leadership Facilitator community where I can be myself and regain hope and capacity as I step back out into the world with this work, the community at New Ventures West where I became an Integral Coach, KK Law for his ability to draw out the essence of the business and to create the web and branding infrastructure to support it, Saskia Wolsak, Editor, for her support to help me clarify my thoughts and written words, Carolyn Sheltraw for her design creativity for the book cover and interior, and the many clients—individuals, teams and organizations—with whom I have had the honor to work with over the years.

Now I have become myself. It's taken
Time, many years and places,
I have been dissolved and shaken,
Worn other people's faces,
Run madly, as if Time were there,
Terribly old, crying a warning.
"Hurry, you will be dead before –"
(What? Before you reach the morning?
Or the end of the poem is clear?
Or love safe in the walled city?)
Now to stand still, to be here,
Feel my own weight and density!...
O, in this single hour I live
All of myself and do not move
I, the pursued, who madly ran,
Stand still, stand still and stop the Sun!

Source: Now I Become Myself, by May Sarton,
quoted in "A Path with Heart", Jack Kornfield, p 208.

TABLE OF CONTENTS

FOREWORD:

San Diego, CA. It was a sunny Friday morning in February 1999, and I was lying on the floor of a bedroom having blacked out. Two times I tried to standup and shake it off and both times I blacked out again. I crawled back into bed and called my girlfriend at the time, a nurse at San Diego Children's Hospital, to ask for her help. It took me three days to feel "normal" again.

Several months went by with a complete battery of tests from blood work to heart EKGs and treadmill stress tests. All of them came back fine and of course they did, I worked out seven days a week, ate a very strict healthy diet, didn't drink that much and never touched drugs or smoked; I considered my body a temple. Knowing that didn't help my denial. The reality was at 27 years old my life was spinning out of control and I was burnt out.

How I got there is a long story but let's just say a Type A personality, a series of non-values based goals set at 18 (President of a company, certain salary, house, car, travel, you name it) all to be achieved by 30 (and completed by 27), might have had something to do with it. My life on paper was perfect but I wasn't happy, I couldn't tell anyone why, and frankly, who would listen?

It took a while but that wake-up call set the course for the past 13 years of my life: a life that puts *me* ahead of my ambitions, and my values, purpose, and authenticity at the center of what matters to me.

Eight years into that journey I had the pleasure of meeting Tana, and for the past five years we've been peers, co-collaborators, kindred spirits, coaches, mentors, protégés, and most importantly, friends. It's been said that on the journey to find who you truly are some very special people will come into your life and help guide you through the learning you need. Tana is one of those people for me; it's truly been an honour and a pleasure.

Even with all of that, at the age of 39, after the death of my father and having pulled my company through the recession, I was sitting in a naturopath's office hearing that I had adrenal fatigue, basically the hormonal manifestation of burnout. All I thought to myself was, "not again."

When Tana first starting talking about Authentic Leadership I have to admit that I didn't truly know what she was talking about: authenticity, I get that, leadership, yes, I'm in that business so I get that too. What I've come to learn from her and watched her model in her life, is in the pages of this book. What I can tell you is that the authentic leader in you has always existed, is in you right now, is who you truly are, and who you were always meant to be. If that is "what" an authentic leader is, then this book is the "how."

Whether, like me, you come to a crisis point in your life, or you feel like you have plateaued, or you are at the top of your game and feel like something is missing, or you just feel lost and know if you could only have a little help in the right direction, this book is for you. Once you start experiencing this book an awakening will most likely come over you and like glitter, once you have it, it sticks. As Tana says in Chapter Four, once the awakening occurs, you can either act on it or ignore it, but either way, it's not going away.

As you begin this journey you will learn that there are three foundational behaviours that support authenticity. By practicing these on an ongoing basis, you will have more capacity to stand in your truth and to be authentic in the moment. These behaviours provide a starting point for every leader who chooses to live aligned with their Authentic Self. And what I know to be true is that by practicing new behaviours over time your beliefs subtly start to shift at the same time; what is a new behaviour becomes a habit, and finally, once internalized, ceases to be a habit and becomes who you are.

Authentic Leadership is both a journey and the destination. I hope you enjoy "doing" this book as much as I did.

Warm regards,
Mike Desjardins
Driver (CEO)
ViRTUS
www.virtusinc.com

INTRODUCTION

AN IDEA WHOSE TIME HAS COME

Have you ever been on the cusp of an idea whose time has come? You read about it for the first time—introduced in a single thought or article. Then it begins to spring up in unexpected places. Skeptics begin to question it. Next it is being talked about across different contexts. And finally it becomes the norm and is embraced by the mainstream. People can't remember what life was like without it.

Authentic Leadership is an idea whose time has come.

Business leaders have finally come to the understanding that in order to be successful it's important to care about people who work within an organization, as well as the customers they serve. Even more, it's essential.

A focus on emotional and social intelligence has exploded. Organizational leaders are looking to the next frontier, facilitating continuous innovation by engaging the hearts of employees, and creating exceptional customer experiences and, thereby driving the ever-important bottom line.

Challenges to achieve this vision abound. Staying ethical is a constant issue. Sincerely supporting employees while meeting growth targets creates daily operating tensions.

The current Holy Grail is how to efficiently foster creativity and innovation when employees are stressed and overloaded. The world is rife with organizational cultures in which employers manage by fear, expecting employees to overwork and neglect their wellness. The time has come to create a new norm!

Daniel Pink, in his book *Drive*[1] talks about the need for a new operating system in business—one that is purpose driven, in addition to being

---

[1]   Daniel Pink, DRiVE—the *Surprising Truth About What Motivates Us*. (New York: River Head Books; The Penguin Group, 2009) p 77, 90, 111, 133.

3

profit driven; one in which employees experience more meaning, are encouraged to practice self-mastery, and are given the autonomy they crave.

Daniel Goleman, in his many books and articles on emotional and social intelligence, calls for leaders to understand and manage their inner experiences and to engage intrinsic motivation for more effective external behaviours.

Authenticity is the bridge to this new world.

Authentic Leadership was introduced to mainstream business in February 2007 with Bill George's article "Discover Your Authentic Leadership," and later with his groundbreaking book *True North*. In March of the same year, an entire issue of Oprah Winfrey's magazine was dedicated to the importance of authenticity for positive personal impact and a meaningful life. Since then, countless conversations have been started, and companies formed to help individuals and corporate leaders around the world to be themselves, to connect with their values, and to bring more meaning into their leadership and their lives.

While the usual way business has been conducted has been successful, gaps are showing up; the context has changed. Natural resources are dwindling, the environment is at risk, the marketplace is global for more companies than it has ever been, virtual workplaces mean declining levels of personal contact and connection, and social engagement is creating a level of accountability that will continue to reinforce the need for ethical behaviour in organizations.

New leadership practices are emerging to fill the need. These can be thought of much like the holistic healthcare movement that is providing complementary offerings for mainstream medical practices. Such leadership practices include the following:

- Mindfulness and meditation have emerged as practices to support accessing, at will, the high-performance, or awakened mind.[2]
- There is a movement to let go of multi-tasking in order be present and focus on one thing at a time. Imagine that! For years the focus in organizations has been on promoting efficiency through juggling multiple balls in the air at one time. The trade-off has, in many cases, been a decrease in quality—in personal interactions, as well as in the company's product and services.
- Somatic or physical practices are being integrated into leadership programs in order to reestablish the connection between mind,

---

2   Anna Wise, *The High-Performance Mind – Mastering Brainwaves for Insight, Healing, and Creativity*. 2nd ed. (New York: Tarcher/Penguin, 1995), p 1.

heart and body, for improved decision making. Leaders are often disconnected from their emotions and their ability to sense what is going on in others—two essential competencies for having empathy and building long-term relationships.

- On the cover of Harvard Business Review's magazine in February 2012 was a large, yellow happy face, along with the title "How Happy Employees Drive Profits." The idea that happiness—true, meaningful happiness—matters, and that leaders are accountable for creating environments that foster engaged and healthy employees, is an important realization.
- Google is focused on cultivating compassion;[3] conferences like Wisdom 2.0 Summit[4] that bring leaders of hi-tech firms such as Facebook, Twitter, Google, eBay and Cisco together with spiritual leaders including Eckhart Tolle and Jack Kornfield—are springing up. Their objective? To make the world a better place through meditation and mindfulness practices.
- Leaders are being told by the big-six consulting firm McKinsey and Company[5], to practice more effective listening, and to support their teams to dig deep and be clear about what truly motivates them.

In a survey on Linked-In by Manie Bosman, CEO of Strategic Leadership Institute, he asked the question, "What is the single most important quality of an effective leader?"[6] The survey closed February 22, 2012 and had 1,494 responders. While purist statisticians can debate the statistical significance, the answers were immediate and clear.

- Emotional and social intelligence—38%
- Vision: inspiring picture of the future—29%
- Communication: skilled communicator—15%
- Competence: knowledge and skills—11%
- Compassion: putting people first—6%

---

3   Tan Chade-Meng, *Everyday Compassion at Google*. TED Talks Video, http://www.youtube.com/watch?v=yTR4sAD_4qM, posted April 2011. http://www.ted.com/talks/lang/eng/chade_meng_tan_everyday_compassion_at_google.html

4   *Wisdom 2.0 Conference* http://wisdom2summit.com/

5   Bernard T. Ferarri, The Executive's Guide to Better Listening, *McKinsey Quarterly*, Feb, 2012. http://www.mckinseyquarterly.com/Governance/Leadership/The_executives_guide_to_better_listening_2931

6   Manie Bosman, "What is the single most important quality of an effective leader?" *Linked In Survey* (Link lost), Feb 22, 2012.

Each of these traits can be developed by practicing authenticity as described in this book, particularly emotional and social intelligence.

Authentic leaders are clear about their vision for the future—both for their own lives as well as for their company. They have exceptional relationship skills as they sincerely care about others. They set a course, and with unwavering determination based on deeply held personal convictions, they move forward. Those around them, magnetized by the authentic leader's humble, grounded way of being, choose to follow. Overlay this with a highly intelligent, technically knowledgeable, and professional person, and you have a very powerful leader.

Authentic Leadership is an idea whose time has come.

WHAT THIS BOOK IS ABOUT

Once the idea of authenticity is presented a number of questions arise: What is authenticity? What is Authentic Leadership? Why make the investment? What are the returns? And, most importantly: How do leaders become authentic? What is the process involved? What are the practical steps and tools they can use? These are the questions addressed in this book. In it you'll learn the following:

- What Authentic Leadership is
- The ROI on an organization's investment in authentic leaders
- The three Cs of an authentic leader
- The four steps of becoming authentic
- What inner development involves
- How managing your inner development supports more effective leadership behaviours
- How the Authentic You™ Personal Planning System supports awakening and personal clarity
- How to put this system into practice
- How a community of support is essential for your development
- How to celebrate results and course-correct to support the ebb and flow of your life

WHAT MAKES THIS BOOK UNIQUE

This book differs from other leadership development and goal-setting books in two main ways—it begins with Authentic Self, and it focuses on inner development as a foundation for more effective experiences.

It starts with Authentic Self

First, it starts with a reconnection to Authentic Self—who you are when at your best.

As you work through the exercises in this book and develop greater awareness, you will begin to remember and experience more of who you truly are. This process can release you from the routine thoughts and behaviors based on unhelpful aspects of your personality—thoughts and behaviors that are just a subset of your true potential. By reconnecting to the emotions you feel when accepting who you are at your best, you will develop a new perspective on your life.

When you apply this perspective to your leadership principles and behaviours, amazing things will begin to occur for yourself and others around you.

When leading with authenticity you will meet challenging situations with greater awareness; you will be able to stop and choose how to respond to your emotions, and, rather than using automatic or default responses (often based on past experiences), you will be able to choose different, more appropriate ways forward.

You will begin to allow other people to experience more of you as you learn to be real in how you interact with them. You will have more perspective in difficult situations: conversations about performance, culturally new situations, and situations where creativity, innovation and new paradigms are being called for. You will be able to collaborate and co-create where once there was only competition. You will also learn to embrace community in order to experience meaningful relationships with others.

Your business will be supported as creativity is unleashed and employees become more engaged, or re-engaged. They will be able to let down their guard and be themselves as well, as they experience authenticity through your way of being. The more relaxed and focused the individual, the more productive the teams.

It focuses on inner development

The second way this book is different from others is that it is focused on the awareness that there are inner experiences occurring at the same time as the external career and life journey. Inner development includes understanding and managing how your mind works: your thoughts, emotions and what you are sensing; as well as how your personality is impacting your leadership—both positively and negatively. It also includes understanding the basics of neuroscience and how the brain can be supporting, or getting in the way of, authenticity.

This book provides a practical system and activities for understanding and managing your inner development in order to achieve better results in the external realm. For example, a simple shift regarding a belief about not being able to trust a team member, or the need to have complete control, can support more effective delegation. This results in both improved business results and higher levels of engagement. In addition, it creates the conditions for all employees to achieve results while experiencing personal meaning, as they are encouraged to live authentically.

Think of the Authentic You™ Personal Planning System as a form of personal strategic planning that supports continuous focus on leading and living aligned with your Authentic Self. It is a simple system that is useful to create inner clarity for all leaders for the rest of their lives. It starts with remembering Authentic You™, and includes elements of both external and inner development. It provides inner guidance for more effective external behaviours and experiences. It supports a customized approach based on the uniqueness of each person and their path in life. And it provides a way to incorporate the learnings from the many resources available for a customized approach to personal and leadership development.

EVERYONE CAN BE A LEADER

In this book, the word "leader" is given a very broad definition. The benefits of leading authentically are equally applicable to leaders outside of the corporate world—whether parents, volunteers leading a community program, expats living in a new country who want to embrace the culture while remaining true to themselves, or teens who want to stand in their truth.

An authentic leader is any person whose life and leadership is guided by a strong inner clarity about the right thing to do. An authentic leader lives and leads in alignment with their Authentic Self—who they are when at their best. They are clear about their ethics and unique way to help others; they make life-affirming or powerful choices[7] to make the organization, community and world a better place.

While this version of the book is written for a person in an organization, you don't need to be the CEO to be a leader.

---

7   As opposed to life-destructing or Forceful choices, as defined by David Hawkins and outlined in Chapter 10 – Truth, Consciousness and Authenticity.

WHOM THIS BOOK WILL SUPPORT

This book is for you if you are ready to take your leadership and your life to the next level. It is for women and men, anywhere in the world, who have reached a time in their lives when they have had a wake-up call of some kind, they want to take their leadership to the next level, or they are searching for more meaning.

You may sense that something is not quite right in the way you lead. You may be a technically excellent leader with a high IQ, who has a difficult time with relationships. Or you may be a new leader who has just entered the corporate world and is trying to fit yourself into an image of leadership you believe to be the right one, and yet it takes so much effort that you are burning out. The one thing readers have in common is that you want to connect to who you are and live more of your life aligned with your purpose. And you are looking to understand the "how". How to be authentic, and what practical support and tools can help you to achieve your goal.

HOW TO USE THIS BOOK TO SUPPORT
AUTHENTIC LEADERSHIP

This book provides a system for individual self-directed learning within an organizational context.

The first six chapters provide an overview of the philosophy of Authentic Leadership—what it is, why it is important, and how leaders can become authentic. Chapter seven connects the dots between authenticity and emotional and social intelligence.

Chapter eight provides a detailed overview of the nine steps of the Authentic You™ Personal Planning System. Each step includes an overview of concepts and processes. Chapter nine is how to put it all into practice. Chapter ten shows how authenticity supports global consciousness. And the author shares her personal journey in the Afterword. Action worksheets are also provided (see Appendix A) with simple exercises to help you see new possibilities, create new habits, and build new skills to be authentic.

Throughout the book, references are made to the website www.leadauthentic.com in which you can find materials, programs and other resources to support you as you begin your journey to becoming an authentic leader.

CHAPTER ONE:
WHAT IS AN
AUTHENTIC LEADER?

*Relax into your authenticity and live
this day with just a little more ease.*

The focus of this book is largely about the "How"—how can a leader become authentic? In order to set the context, though, it is first helpful to understand the "What"—What is Authentic Self? What is an authentic leader? What are the key characteristics of an authentic leader?

WHAT IS AUTHENTIC SELF?

In order to understand Authentic Self, it is helpful to discuss another, often more dominant, aspect of our minds - our personality. By learning to distinguish between the two, authentic leaders develop the important understanding that their potential is broader than what they are currently aware of.

They may be aware of their strengths, and they may also be aware of their opportunities to be more effective. They may have noticed, for example, a tendency to react too quickly, or to interpret situations incorrectly, and the impact this has had on themselves and others.

Leaders may also be unaware of aspects of themselves that are undiscovered or, more accurately, have been forgotten—joy, compassion, creativity, as well as the ability to be clear and firm; aspects of authenticity that have been covered up by layers of personality.

11

By developing awareness of habitual ways of thinking as well as forgotten, and possibly more joyful, ways of seeing the world, a leader can start to differentiate between personality and Authentic Self.

Authentic Self is who you are when at your best—a creative and compassionate person with the unique qualities that make you who you are. Authentic Self is guided by intrinsic motivation, personal clarity, and ethics. It is your potential and your birthright.

According to Don Richard Riso and Russ Hudson, our Essence (or as we call it our Authentic Self) is "....what we fundamentally are, our Essential Self." They also describe it as "an individual spark of the Divine, although we have forgotten this fundamental truth because we have fallen asleep to our true nature."[8]

Personality includes the aspects of self that develop from birth to adulthood as a result of influences and experiences in your life. Some aspects of personality are helpful (strengths) and others are no longer benefiting you (self-limiting thoughts and beliefs).

According to Riso and Hudson, personality is "the familiar, conditioned parts of a much wider range of potentials that we all possess."[9]

---

8   Don Richard Riso and Russ Hudson, *The Wisdom of the Enneagram - The Complete Guide to Psychological and Spiritual Growth for the Nine Personality Types* (New York: A Bantham Book, 1999), p 27.

9   Ibid.

Authentic Self vs. Personality

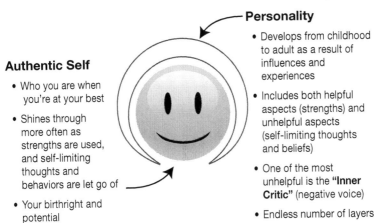

Personality

- Develops from childhood to adult as a result of influences and experiences

- Includes both helpful aspects (strengths) and unhelpful aspects (self-limiting thoughts and beliefs)

- One of the most unhelpful is the **"Inner Critic"** (negative voice)

- Endless number of layers

Authentic Self

- Who you are when you're at your best

- Shines through more often as strengths are used, and self-limiting thoughts and behaviors are let go of

- Your birthright and potential

Source: enneagraminsitute.com/articles/NArtEgoAndEssence.asp

The distinction between Authentic Self and personality has also been likened to a set of Russian dolls where as you remove the top off one, another and another appears within until finally the one at the centre is left; a diamond that has become dusty; or a clear windowpane on which layers of dirt have accumulated over many years.

The images are many, though the idea is consistent. Beneath the layers of personality lives the true nature of the person—the Authentic Self—always there and waiting to be rediscovered and remembered. The number of layers of personality, particularly those that are unhelpful or unhealthy, depends on many factors including genetics, upbringing, culture, and lifestyle.

Generally, we do not experience our Essence and its many aspects because our awareness is so dominated by our personality. But as we learn to bring awareness to our personality, it becomes more transparent, and we are able to experience our Essence more directly.[10]

Our Authentic Self shines through more often as we understand and engage our strengths, see the self-limiting thoughts and beliefs for what they are, and let them go in order to make choices aligned with who we truly are.

---

10   Ibid.

WHAT IS AN AUTHENTIC LEADER?

Before discussing what an authentic leader is, it can be helpful to first define what a leader is and then to clarify the distinction.

WHAT IS A LEADER?

A leader is anyone who steps forward and influences others, and whom others choose to follow.

In an organization every employee has the potential to be a leader, whether they are a CEO, an experienced manager or a company's most recent arrival.

Leadership also exists in other parts of our lives. A leader can be a volunteer, a friend, a teen or a parent. For the purposes of this book, however, we will focus on leaders in an organizational context.

WHAT IS AN AUTHENTIC LEADER?

An Authentic Leader is a person whose life and leadership is guided by a strong inner clarity about the right thing to do.

Margaret Wheatley, in her book Leadership and the New Sciences, discusses the need for leaders to develop different ways for the future and the importance of a new way of thinking, or new consciousness:

> I believe that we have only just begun the process of discovering and inventing the new organizational forms that will inhabit the 21st century. To be responsible inventors and discoverers, we need the courage to let go of the old world, to relinquish most of what we have cherished, to abandon our interpretations about what does and doesn't work. We must learn to see the world anew. As Einstein is often quoted as saying: No problem can be solved from the same consciousness that created it.

Authentic leaders can provide this new way!

An authentic leader lives and leads in alignment with their Authentic Self—who they are when at their best. They are clear about their ethics and unique way to help others; they make life-affirming or powerful choices to make the organization, community and world a better place.

In addition to having a drive for results and technical and professional excellence, an authentic leader has an inspiring way of being that others can sense and may not be able to describe.

THE FOUR CS OF AN AUTHENTIC LEADER

There are four characteristics of an authentic leader—clear, choiceful, consistent, and caring. Each is described below.

1. Clear

Authentic Leaders are guided by a strong personal or inner clarity—an inner guidance system (think GPS) that is made up of different components.

First, they are clear about who they are. This includes their Authentic Self, their strengths as well as the self-limiting thoughts and beliefs of their personality.

Next, they are clear about what they believe in. They have taken the time to articulate their values and to understand boundaries around what is acceptable to them. They also understand what their higher purpose is—what they believe they are on this earth to do with their life.

Authentic leaders are clear about how they want to live and lead. They have thought about and clarified their vision for their life, including both the personal and the business. They have defined the principles they follow for their day-to-day leadership of self and others. They may set goals or they may set intentions. Either way, they are open to the steps that arise that guide them towards achieving their life vision.

2. Choiceful[11]

Authentic leaders make intentional choices based on personal or inner clarity. They take a proactive role in the creation of their life. Each choice they make can be checked against what they know to be true. If it is not aligned with their Authentic Self, their values or their vision, they choose differently.

In addition, authentic leaders are choiceful about whom they are in relationship with and how they support others. They understand how to make choices to create optimal conditions for those around them to flourish and be themselves as well.

---

11   Choiceful—we've decided to create a new word—one that is helpful for discussing Authentic Leaders.

3. Consistent

Authentic leaders are consistent in a number of ways. First, they are genuine and the same in all parts of their life. They feel no need to wear a mask in order to be successful and fit in at work. They are grounded and humble through highs and lows. They enjoy giving credit to others for a team effort they have been involved in. They immediately accept responsibility when errors or difficulties occur. They have no need to be the centre of attention and are comfortable with who they are.

Authentic leaders are also consistent in situations that get intense, responding calmly and clearly regardless of the challenge. If a new employee, for example, comes to them with a mistake, authentic leaders practice patience and empathy; if a bully behaves aggressively towards authentic leaders, they clearly and firmly set a boundary and/or end the relationship. If they once were perceived as a bully themselves, they have worked through this personal issue – they have developed awareness and practices to override this unhelpful impulse and to choose to practice empathy and grounded leadership.

Authentic leaders have the awareness and skill to self-manage and maintain their composure and perspective. Because of their consistent and approachable way of being, they are able to build a strong foundation of trust in their relationships with others.

4. Caring

And finally, authentic leaders are caring. They have learned to care about themselves, as well as others—an aspect of leadership that is sometimes overlooked.

One of the most unhelpful aspects of personality is the negative voice that plays over and over in the mind and gets in the way of experiencing our Authentic Self. It is called the "inner critic." Authentic leaders understand the inner critic and its impact on themselves and others. They are able to see it for what it is—a series of unhelpful thoughts or sensations that arises as a result of past experiences—and to let its influence go, more of the time.

By learning to manage the inner critic, they can begin to care more for themselves. Once they can have self-compassion, authentic leaders have greater desire and ability to care more for others. The ability to have empathy is essential for working effectively with others—whether peers, direct reports, clients or stakeholders. It is foundational to creating environments where others can flourish.

Authentic leaders take the time to enjoy being in relationship with those around them. They can override the impacts of a very full schedule, plus impatience and frustration, in order to be fully present in their interactions, adding a level of quality and depth to each.

Appropriate vulnerability, backed up by caring for their self, is an incredible strength of authentic leaders. While some will judge it as a sign of weakness, leaders become more approachable to others when they practice letting their guard down. By being vulnerable and sharing their growth opportunities, they model for others that it is okay for their development to be a work in progress. Teammates can become more compassionate with themselves knowing that it is normal for them to have issues to work on too.

And finally, authentic leaders understand the interconnectedness of all things, and are dedicating their lives to helping make the organization, the community, and the world a better place to be.

SUMMARY

The focus of this book is how to become an authentic leader. An Authentic Leader is a person whose life and leadership are guided by a strong personal or inner clarity about the right thing to do. They live and lead in alignment with Authentic Self—who they are when at their best. They are clear about their ethics and unique way to help others; they make life-affirming or powerful choices[12] to make the organization, community and world a better place.

In addition to having a drive for business results as well as technical and professional excellence, authentic leaders have four characteristics, called the 4Cs: they are clear, choiceful, consistent and caring.

---

12   Ibid, David Hawkins and outlined in Chapter 10 – Truth, Consciousness and Authenticity.

CHAPTER TWO:
WHAT IS THE BUSINESS CASE FOR AUTHENTIC LEADERSHIP IN ORGANIZATIONS?

When paired with technical and professional excellence, authenticity provides a unique business advantage for leaders in the 21st century.

THE NEXT FRONTIER FOR LEADERSHIP

One of the biggest opportunities facing organizations today is that of improving business results by supporting all employees to live their full potential.

Technical and professional excellence, a drive for results, and a team of high-achievers will take a company so far. A huge leverage point is to develop authenticity in every person across a company.

Experienced leaders begin their research into new ideas with the question "What's the business case?" The business case for Authentic Leadership is outlined below and includes:

- The Deliverables
- The Investment
- The Return on Investment (ROI)

A. The Deliverables

The first deliverable includes more effective leaders who are able to manage themselves as well as create environments for others to live their potential. By doing so they directly improve business results.

The second deliverable is the improved effectiveness, focus and engagement of the employees positively impacted by the authentic leaders.

B. The Investment

The investment for each authentic leader requires an individualized approach to learning and development. Learning with the emotional centre of the brain[13], which is what authenticity requires, takes more time than conventional formal learning, requires a tailored approach, targeted guidance where needed, and ongoing conversations with others on a similar journey.

Each leader's development plan is customized based on who they are, where they start their journey, and their unique opportunities for development (strengths and self-limiting beliefs).

Developing authenticity includes years of practice, beginning with an initial awakening. With curiosity and openness, an authentic leader can learn something new about themselves every day for the rest of their life. And as they practice, their authenticity unfolds and takes hold.

The investment also includes participating in a community of support. Authenticity can be fragile or inconsistent, as one must develop the ability to be authentic in different kinds of situations and with people of different personality types. Having a safe place to practice being authentic is essential—a place to understand and support others, as well as to receive guidance when needed. Leaders may require several communities of support at the same time, or at different times, over the course of their lives.

C. The ROI

The Return on Investment (ROI) includes improved results—both for the business, as well as for the community, and even beyond to the world. Leaders who are authentic have improved emotional and social intelligence, exceptional relationship skills and the ability to create great environments where others can flourish. They are also aware of the ripple effect and indirect impacts of their personal authenticity.

---

13   Daniel Goleman, "What Makes a Leader?", *Harvard Business Review,* (http://hbr. org/2004/01/what-makes-a-leader/ar/1, 1998), p 5.

HIGH LEVELS OF EMOTIONAL AND SOCIAL INTELLIGENCE

Emotional and social intelligence as outlined in the work of Daniel Goleman[14], includes five components—self-awareness, self-regulation (or self-management), motivation, empathy and social skills.

Authentic leaders constantly evolve their emotional and social intelligence and it shows up in a number of ways. First, awareness of new aspects of themselves occurs daily and they are able to manage their emotions in the moment, particularly in intense or new situations. Next they are able to balance their motivation—considering both what is important to them from an intrinsic or internal perspective, as well as what is important from the extrinsic or external. They take action, both because they know that it aligns with their values and is the right thing to do, and because it aligns with their business goals.

Daniel Pink identifies a new operating system required for business success—one that places a high level of value on intrinsic motivation. Internally motivated individuals focus on three things: first, they practice mastery, over time, of a subject important to them; second, they are given autonomy to choose the right path to achieve an outcome; and third, they feel their work is connected to a higher purpose beyond the company.

> ...the profit motive, potent though it is, can be an insufficient impetus for both individuals and organizations. An equally powerful source of energy, one we've often neglected or dismissed as unrealistic, is what we might call the purpose motive. [15]

Pink sees a new operating system—Motivation 3.0—as essential to business success as, "it doesn't reject profits, but it places equal emphasis on Purpose maximization" in "goals, words and policies."[16]

Authentic leaders have a clear sense of their intrinsic motivators and this provides them with meaning and purpose. This personal clarity also supports strong ethics and an understanding of their vision for their life. In addition, they have the awareness and ability to check in on their motivation when unsure of the next step or when something doesn't feel right.

---

14   Goleman, "What Makes a Leader?", p 1.

15   Pink, Drive, pp. 134-135.

16   Ibid.

That is, as well as gathering information from others, they look within to ensure alignment with Authentic Self. If something isn't aligned, a different choice is made.

EXCEPTIONAL RELATIONSHIP SKILLS

Authentic leaders have exceptional relationship skills. They build long-term, trust-based relationships. They foster a high level of quality in both face-to-face and virtual interactions, by practicing being present and focusing their attention.

People want to be around authentic leaders. Others feel comfortable to be themselves and this can be an unusual experience for many employees in organizations. These leaders can tap into empathy and practice it even when they have to override impatience and frustration. And they can quickly get a sense for how another person is experiencing an interaction and establish rapport in order to build trust.

Authentic leaders have a realistic confidence and ability to navigate any situation by drawing on their internal sense of what is true. They are humble and grounded and their energy resonates for others to the point that others calm down when around them.

Being authentic doesn't mean being soft.

It can mean being clear and firm where it is appropriate. Authentic leaders have an understanding of what their boundaries are and can set one in the moment when they need to.

And finally, they have the ability to navigate successfully through difficulties in relationships, knowing that both ups and downs will arise over time. Their intentions for long-term relationships support them to maintain perspective and remember another's good intentions as well. They see every difficult situation as an opportunity to renew and strengthen a relationship or become aware of when it is important to let one go.

THE ABILITY TO CREATE OPTIMAL ENVIRONMENTS FOR IMPROVED BUSINESS RESULTS

An authentic leader is able to create optimal environments for others to flourish, resulting in improved business results in a number of different areas.

Indeed, superior results over a sustained period of time is the ultimate mark of an authentic leader. It may be possible to drive short-term outcomes without being authentic, but Authentic Leadership is the only way we know to create sustainable long-term results.[17]

When employees are relaxed and comfortable around their boss—as opposed to being intimidated or afraid—they are able to tap into their creativity and can be more innovative. Understanding the business advantage of a healthy organization means that authentic leaders will foster it in both themselves and others.

A strong foundation of wellness means that individuals can maintain their perspective through all kinds of situations and can bring themselves back into balance more quickly when they find themselves overwhelmed.

A longing for community is showing up in unexpected places. Facebook, and other social networking sites such as Google +, Twitter, Linked-In and Pinterest, provide examples of ways people want to be in community, that are different than in the past. Connections are made with others around the world on a day-to-day basis and can be focused on a topic of mutual interest.

In many organizations there is a paradox in community. While employees want community, they often isolate, particularly when under stress, and feel they need to come up with solutions on their own. When they embrace being on a team, however, they can work more effectively—synergies arise and solutions are often more effective than what they would have been if created alone.

Community is essential for authenticity, providing a safe place for you to dip into again and again to receive support, provide support, develop skills and learn about yourself with others who are living and leading authentically.

Customers have a different experience with people who are authentic. When a trusted supplier or consultant, who has exceptional relationship skills, in addition to technical proficiency, is sought out for guidance, the customer can relax. The supplier creates the conditions for the client to have a good experience in every interaction as value is delivered.

Authentic leaders support employees to be their personal best and to bring their Authentic Self to their work. These employees are more engaged as a result.

---

17   Bill George, and Peter Sims, Andrew N. McLean, and Diana Mayer, "Discovering Your Authentic Leadership." *Harvard Business Review,* Volume 85: No 2 (February 2007), p 138.

Engaged employees are 40% more productive than those who are disengaged; they are also 85% less likely to leave an organization, which also minimizes costs of turnover.[18]

Authentic leaders can motivate and engage employees as they take the time to listen and understand the other person's perspective. Leaders come into a relationship with positional credibility—they are the boss—which creates an immediate power imbalance that can intimidate employees. Mature leaders are aware of this and model authenticity. This creates an environment where employees and others around them feel safe to be themselves —to be creative, to challenge assumptions, and to take initiative.

FAR-REACHING IMPACTS

Authentic leaders are clear about their ethics, and how they will do their part to make the world a better place.

This is reflected in their purpose and how they make choices to live it every day. They have a positive impact on others that extends beyond an organization.

When others experience an authentic leader's way of being, and they begin a practice for themselves, the benefits extend to the family, the community and beyond to the world.

Never underestimate the positive ripple effect you can have every day and how that is strengthened by being authentic.

SUMMARY

The next frontier for leadership development is for organizations to support every employee to realize more of their potential by fostering authenticity. The business case for authenticity includes the deliverables, the investment and the return on investment. The deliverables include better leaders and more engaged employees because of the great environments these leaders create. The investment involves a customized approach to learning and continuous practice for personal development. It also includes creating communities of support where authentic leaders can gather to seek

---

18   "Driving Employee Performance and Retention Through Engagement – A Qualitative Analysis of the effectiveness of Employee Engagement Strategies." *Corporate Leadership Council,* Corporate Executive Board, 2004.

and provide guidance and to "recharge" before going back into their day-to-day leadership to practice being authentic in more situations. The return on investment includes improved emotional and social intelligence including exceptional relationship skills, the ability to create great environments where employees can flourish, and a positive ripple effect that can extend out to the community and world.

CHAPTER THREE:
HOW DO LEADERS BECOME AUTHENTIC?

Every moment of each day brings a
new opportunity to practice being authentic.

AUTHENTICITY AS A LIFE-LONG JOURNEY

Authentic leaders see life as a journey where each day brings new opportunities to practice being authentic.

This journey involves four recurring steps: An initial **awakening**, with tension that builds as you experience an aspect of yourself that is different than what you believe. Next you develop a greater **awareness** of your internal and external experiences. By understanding and sometimes managing the inner goings on, you will have more choice in how you experience the world and in your behaviours. Sometimes there are differences between what is occurring internally and your intent in the situation. To improve your leadership effectiveness by reconciling any incongruence that may occur between your inner experiences and your behaviours, **action** is required. With action, the next level of **awareness** arises, and leads to the next awakening.

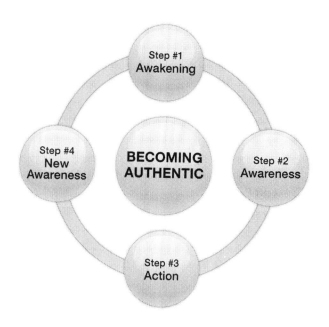

The process is cyclical, generating ever-increasing levels of authenticity and awareness. While in this description we begin with an awakening, it is important to recognize that the process can also begin with awareness—glimpses of the self that add up until they create an awakening of substantial proportion that leads to further awareness and a need for action.

Example: a manager notices that he is having a difficult time staying focused when his email is on and he can hear the "ping" when he gets mail. As soon as he hears this signal, he is in the habit of changing his focus to react to the email, rather than completing the conversation or task at hand. After several weeks of noticing this about himself, he awakens to the fact that his quality of work is being impacted by his habit of losing focus at the beck and call of his email ping. The awakening is followed by an awareness of the impact of the tension he holds in his shoulders when he works on email, and eye strain as well. This awareness leads to the need for action and the manager learns to self-manage and let go of his habit of reacting to email. He builds capacity to stay present to the conversation or task at hand and the quality improves. His stress level diminishes as he begins to turn his email off for periods of time when he requires concentration and creativity.

INTERNAL EXPERIENCES GUIDE EXTERNAL EXPERIENCES

The journey to becoming authentic involves understanding that you are having both internal and external experiences at the same time, and that the internal determines, in part, the external. Authentic leaders understand and manage both their inner and outer experiences through inner development and personal growth.

Starting Now

Authenticity can be a part of your journey at any stage of your life. When you begin will depend on the timing of your initial awakening and if and when you choose to heed it.

Buddhist nun Pema Chödrön, in her book *Start Where You Are—a Guide to Compassionate Living*[19] talks about starting a journey of compassion now, wherever you are in your life. The same is true for becoming an authentic leader.

You are Whole and Perfect Right Now

Pema Chodron introduces the concept of thinking about yourself as whole and having everything you need right now, as opposed to believing you are flawed and needing to be better or fix your self.

Authenticity assumes a person is whole and merely needs to remember—or experience for the first time—their Authentic Self that may be hidden by unhelpful aspects of their personality. This is why I remind clients to, "Relax into your authenticity and live this day with just a little more ease."

PERSONAL RESPONSIBILITY FOR YOUR JOURNEY

When you accept responsibility for what you have become awake to, you make a choice to begin your personal journey. You are on your way.

At times the journey is enjoyable and at other times it can be frustrating and even a bit daunting. It is actually more difficult to ignore it—as behaving in a way that is incongruent with who you are takes a lot of energy. All those negative thoughts need to be fabricated and perpetuated with negative emotions. A sense of ease and inner peace arises when thoughts and actions are congruent with Authentic Self. Overall, each thought, belief or

---

19   Chodron, Pema, *Start Where you Are—A Guide to Compassionate Living* (Boston, Mass: Shambhala Classics, 1994), p 1.

behaviour you become awake to, and that you accept and do something about, is an investment in who you are, as well as a chance to become your Authentic Self, more of the time.

PERSONAL GROWTH OVER TIME

The ongoing cycle of awakening, awareness, action and the next level of awareness, increases the frequency with which choices are made in alignment with Authentic Self. This results in improved effectiveness as a leader, through personal growth over time.

Each person's personality has a continuum of developmental levels[20] from unhealthy through average to healthy. The healthier you are as a person, the more effective you will be. Your thoughts and behaviours may change over time based on what is occurring in your life. You will be moving up and down between the developmental levels for your unique personality.

In the diagram below there are two axes. The horizontal axis shows time, and the vertical shows the range of developmental levels.

Personal Growth Over Time

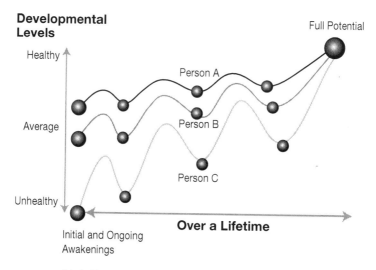

Adapted from: enneagraminsitute.com/articles/NArtEgoAndEssence.asp

---

20   Katy Taylor, "Ego and Essence" *The Enneagram Monthly,* November 2008, Issue 153, http://www.enneagraminstitute.com/articles/NArtEgoAndEssence.asp

CHAPTER THREE: HOW DO LEADERS BECOME AUTHENTIC?

The life-long journey for authenticity involves becoming increasingly healthy to the point of realizing the highest level of potential by living more of each day as your Authentic Self.

Several influences converge to determine the level of development when you have your first awakening. The healthier the upbringing and more positive the early life experiences and influences, and the stronger the foundation of wellness, the healthier the starting point. Conversely, the greater the childhood trauma and the harsher the life-experiences, and/or the lower the level of personal resiliency, the unhealthier the starting point when you experience your initial awakening.

The diagram shows examples of three different life journeys and how each person starts at a different level of development. Each journey begins with the initial awakening and each person can realize his or her potential over time. Person A begins at a healthier level of development than Persons B and C. The steps it takes for each person to realize more of their potential (i.e. Authentic Self) are different and unique. Each person may have several life-altering awakenings along the way. When they heed these, they continue to grow.

Personal growth is experienced as an expansion of your Authentic Self and your strengths, and a relaxation of the unhelpful impacts of personality.

As you become more authentic, you will be able—in the moment—to notice self-limiting thoughts for what they are—simply thoughts or beliefs that you can either listen to or let go of. You will also start to notice when you are being authentic in a situation where you previously were not.

You will experience benefits both internally and externally. It will feel like there is an on and off switch in your mind: Personality or Authentic Self? Asleep or awake? Unconscious or conscious? Which will guide your behaviour in that instant? In each moment, you have a choice.

Over time, the ability to be authentic becomes an integral part of your way of being. You start to make choices with more ease, based on your growing capacity to be your Authentic Self.

Externally your experiences will shift as well. Your behaviours will be more effective as you practice being authentic in more situations.

CHALLENGES AND SUPPORT ALONG THE WAY

On your journey to becoming an authentic leader there will be times when you will walk on your own, and others when it is helpful to seek out the support of guides and mentors.

As you practice being your Authentic Self, you may experience beginner's mind. Some experiences will be uncomfortable as you take time to get used to, and integrate, new ways of thinking and different behaviours into your leadership. There may be low-risk situations in which you feel comfortable and have the capacity to be authentic right away. An example is when you meet with a trusted friend or loved one with whom you can share a newly discovered aspect of your personality. In other situations, people or conversations may trigger you so intensely that you will feel overwhelmed by the level of uncomfortable energy. You may judge these as higher risk situations for you personally and your ability to stay present will be lower than in others. Clearing the discomfort and negative emotions may take hours or even days.

All of this is progress as you continue to develop capacity in different ways at different times.

COMMUNITIES OF SUPPORT

Being authentic takes energy, particularly when it is new. It can be helpful to have one or several Communities of Support where you can gather for an Authenticity Recharge™.

Meeting with others to support, and be supported on your journey to authenticity fosters learning with the emotional centre of the brain, practicing being vulnerable and real. A community of support is like a warm and safe incubator for everyone's capacity for authenticity to grow. This community can include a friend, mentor, or a group. You will feel rejuvenated and regain perspective each time you gather with others to recharge.

SUMMARY

Authenticity is a life-long journey involving four recurring steps—awakening, awareness, action and new awareness. Internal experiences guide external ones. Learning to manage the internal supports improving the effectiveness of the external. You can begin at any time in your life, remembering that you are whole and perfect as you are right now. Becoming authentic means remembering aspects of your true or Authentic Self beyond what you are currently aware. It also involves personal growth over time by evolving to the healthiest developmental level possible—your potential as Authentic Self. A sense of ease arises as the your behaviours are less frequently guided by your personality, and more often by your Authentic Self.

CHAPTER FOUR:
AWAKENING

*Once you have become awake to a
new possibility, you simply can't go back.*

The first step to becoming an authentic leader is to experience an awakening.

An awakening is what occurs when you learn something new about yourself that is startlingly different than what you believe to be true.

Awakenings can be negative or positive and can vary in intensity. You can experience many over your lifetime, each providing an opportunity for choice and growth. The Authentic You™ Personal Planning System provides a way to create an awakening whenever you would like to take your leadership or life to the next level of authenticity and meaning. The System will be introduced in detail in Chapter Eight, though an initial comment is warranted at this time.

The journey begins with an awakening. It is either positive—for example, you were given a promotion and had no idea that it was coming—or it can be not so positive—you receive feedback that something in your style as a leader is no longer working for you (and/or for others).

You receive this information about yourself through feedback—either internally as you wake-up to something different about yourself, or externally from someone else. And you become aware that some of the habitual patterns of thoughts (including beliefs), emotions and/or behaviours that you may have had since childhood, are not conducive to your desired effect.

For example, you learn that you can be experienced as abrupt and aggressive and you have never seen yourself that way. If the significance of the feedback is great enough, it creates an awakening. You suddenly become awake to something in a significant way—at a level you have not been aware of before.

This awakening can be experienced as either positive or negative. If positive, you become awake to a new possibility for how to think about something in your life. For example, you learn that using technology is one of your strengths and you had no awareness of this prior to being given the feedback. Or, if negative, you become awake to an aspect of your style that is impacting yourself and/or others in a way that is unhelpful. For example, you are told that you have a resistance to change that is getting in the way of your moving up in your career.

Awakenings come in two forms. The first is called a wake-up call ("I had no idea I was being perceived that way") and the second is an aha moment ("Aha—now I see a different way of thinking about that....").

WAKE-UP CALLS

Once you have become awake, you can't go back.

Example: you are told you will be fired in 6 months if you are unable to improve your relationships with others. Working with a coach, you become awake to how you think about relationships. You learn that you think about relationships as something that gets in the way of your real work—which you believe is to get things done. This new insight about yourself differs from your self-concept—you believe that you value, and are good at building relationships.

When this feedback is unexpected it can create a sense of anxiousness or tension as you experience a challenge to what you believe to be true about yourself. You are experiencing cognitive dissonance.

WHAT IS COGNITIVE DISSONANCE?

The topic of cognitive dissonance is well known in psychology. Writer Kendra Cherry describes cognitive dissonance as "the feeling of discomfort that results from holding two conflicting beliefs [at one time]. When there is a discrepancy between beliefs and behaviors, something must change in order to eliminate or reduce the dissonance. Cognitive dissonance can occur in many areas of life, but it is particularly evident in situations where an individual's behavior conflicts with beliefs that are integral to his or her self-identity."[21]

Cognitive dissonance can be seen as a wake-up call. It indicates that you have come to a personal fork in the road. You can choose to heed the call and accept it, or push it down and ignore it.

Either way, you are awake now to what is going on for you.

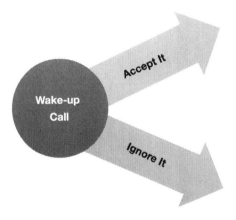

There are implications for each path and the choice is up to you.

Choosing to ignore the wake-up call is one path you can take at the fork in the road. At times you may not be able, or ready, to accept the call. Perhaps the pain of asking for support, or acknowledging the unhelpful aspects of your personality, or revisiting old personal issues, is too painful to even consider.

If you choose to ignore it, the lesson or wake-up call will usually recur, often in a different and more powerful form, until you finally pay attention. In the meantime, you may frantically overfill your life with tasks as it is too uncomfortable to go slow and feel what is really going on. When the wake-up call gets extreme, you may change jobs, relationships and/or even countries in order to try to get away from the discomfort of staying in one place (metaphorically and sometimes literally) to get to know another aspect of your personality.

---

21   Kendra Cherry, *What is Cognitive Dissonance?* http://psychology.about.com/od/cognitivepsychology/f/dissonance.htm, 2012.

The other path is to accept the call. This is when you take responsibility, pay attention to the cognitive dissonance, learn from what is not working in your life, and begin to make conscious, aligned choices.

AHA MOMENTS

Awakenings also occur in the form of aha moments. These occur when you become awake to a new possibility for how to see the world.

You may have a belief about how you are as a leader, or how you need to behave to be successful, and for whatever reason you begin to see the situation in a whole new light.

Example: You are a new manager and you can't see the value of delegating. Your experience is that it takes twice as long to do a task when you need to explain it to someone and teach him or her how to do it, as it would take to just do it yourself.

Your manager sees what is going on for you and shares her experience with you. She explains that she learned to see delegating as both a gift 1) for herself (to create more space to work at the level she needed to work at) as well as 2) for her employees (so they can do more of what they love and are good at; and in turn feel valued and engaged; which leads to higher productivity and quality of results).

You have never thought about delegating like this and her story creates an aha moment—a eureka or solution—that you couldn't see before.

Once you can see a new possibility for the path forward in a situation where you could only see it one way in the past, you can learn how to think and behave differently (in this case how to practice delegating effectively) and improve your leadership.

When you experience an aha moment, you have resolved the cognitive dissonance by evolving your belief or adopting an entirely new one. You may notice a feeling of relief as a solution emerges. You can relax into this new possibility.

AWAKENINGS VARY IN MAGNITUDE

Awakenings vary in intensity and impact.

Sometimes they are strong enough that they shake you to your core and require several months or years to reconcile. Other times they are mild, and a simple adjustment to a thought or behaviour can clear them with minimal discomfort.

THE INITIAL AWAKENING

As mentioned above, your first awakening, when heeded, begins your journey to authenticity. It is intense enough that you simply cannot ignore it. The stakes are made so high for you personally that you must choose to do something differently. Sometimes you can navigate the situation successfully on your own, and sometimes it will require the support of a guide.

ONGOING AWAKENINGS: MAJOR CHANGES

In addition to the initial awakening, there may be other times in your life when major changes occur. These can be positive or negative and could include having a new child, receiving a promotion, getting married or divorced, taking a sabbatical, entering retirement, or experiencing the death of someone important to you. These opportunities for awakening may be just as profound, or even more so, than the first.

The result of every awakening that you heed is a new level of awareness.

You experience an aspect of your personality for what it is—something that, if you continue believing it and behaving in the way it causes you to behave, will limit your ability as a leader. You arrive at a fork in the road, and can choose to live with it (and ignore the wake-up call), or you can learn to shift it and let it go.

Example: Continuing with the earlier example, once you become aware that you habitually see relationships as getting in the way of doing your real work, you may realize that you have maintained a distance in all relationships in your life. One result is that you are experiencing extreme loneliness. Another is that you realize you don't really care about others and your behaviours show it— you are often impatient and lack empathy.

Others experience you as standoffish and arrogant. They have a difficult time working with you. While they respect your work, they "walk on eggshells," not understanding why your manner toward them is short. They may assume they have done something wrong and that they cannot live up to your standards, no matter what quality they bring to their work.

These dynamics, which are common in the corporate world, can be ineffective for engaging employees and creating the conditions for innovation and excellent customer experiences. Imagine the possibilities if more leaders listened to their awakenings.

MILD AWAKENINGS

Mild awakenings occur as small, daily realizations that your habits of thought and behaviour are unhelpful. These awakenings may be less intense as they are a lower risk to your usual lifestyle, and have less of an implication for yourself and others.

It can be nice to know that awakenings don't all have to shake you to your core! All that is required to reconcile these lesser internal conflicts is to self-manage to make a simple shift to your thinking and to choose a more appropriate behaviour. This leads to a different experience and to opportunity for growth on a daily basis.

Example: you learn that your facial expression is incongruent with your intention. People are intimidated by you when you say you are "Fine" and at the same time your tightly crossed arms and indignant tone of voice say you are definitely not fine.

The awareness that you appear intimidating conflicts with your belief that you are effective at reaching others. This creates a mild internal conflict. In this case a simple adjustment—awareness of your impact on others or perhaps verbal acknowledgement of it— is all that is needed. In addition, practicing smiling and relaxing your face, softening the intensity of your eyes, can change your expression and make the other person's experience more congruent with your intention.

After taking responsibility for your internal and external experiences and your impact on others, the key to authenticity is to admit that you may still have some things to learn in life, and commit to being open to continuous awakenings.

SUMMARY

The first step to becoming an authentic leader includes experiencing an awakening. Awakenings can be negative or positive and can vary in intensity. You can experience many over your lifetime and each provides an opportunity for choices and growth. They can arise out of feedback from others, or you can use the Authentic You™ Personal Planning System to create an awakening when you want to take your leadership and life to the next level of authenticity. Wake-up calls are intense awakenings that create cognitive dissonance as you learn something new about your self that is incongruent with what you believe. You can either heed a wake-up call and grow, or choose to ignore it until it shows up again.

Awakenings also show up as aha moments where you become awake to a new possibility or solution. The key to becoming authentic is to be open to learning new things about yourself as awakenings arise.

CHAPTER FIVE:
AWARENESS

Awareness shines a light on the many dimensions of who you are so your Authentic Self can guide your behaviours, more of the time.

The second step to becoming an authentic leader is to cultivate awareness.

Awareness arises as you notice your inner experiences, at the same time as your external ones, and how they impact the experience of others.

The first aspect of awareness is personal or inner clarity—about who you are and what is important to you at this point in your leadership and your life. This is a distinguishing feature of authentic leaders—they lead based on a clear, internal guidance system. While they listen to, and gather information from external sources, they can assess objectively, and within a global, ethical context, what the right thing to do is in each situation.

On your own journey to authenticity, it can be helpful to understand your personal context and to hold this as an internal beacon that guides your choices and behaviours. Your context may include understanding and articulating the following:

Authentic Self: who you are when at your best
Values: deeply held beliefs about what is important to you
Purpose: the higher purpose or what you were meant to contribute in your life

Life vision: *how you want your life to look when you are completely happy*

Leadership principles: *how you translate your Authentic Self, values and life vision, into your day-to-day actions*

Work-life balance: *what the optimal balance in all parts of your life is, versus the current state*

Goals or intentions: *what you would like to focus your efforts on achieving personally and in business, within a certain timeframe*

Inner development plan: *the aspects of personality you would like to let go or the strengths you would like to develop, of in order to lead authentically*

While these components will be discussed in detail in Chapter eight: The Authentic You™ Personal Planning System, it is important to introduce them here. All of these interrelated components make up a system that creates awareness in the form of personal clarity. Once you articulate them for the first time, you have a different perspective or context for living your life. The Authentic You™ Personal Planning System can be used at any time to establish your personal clarity—when you want to take your leadership to the next level; when you have a life change (such as starting a new family); and are unsure of what your next step is; or when opportunities present themselves and you need up-to-date criteria to make the choice.

The second aspect of awareness that authentic leaders practice includes the new levels of awareness that arise continuously each day. This comes about as leaders pay attention to what is occurring in their internal experiences throughout the day—their thoughts, emotions, and what they are sensing. Awareness also extends to their external experiences—their behaviours and how they impact others.

To practice awareness – begin by noticing two things at the same time. First notice what is occurring around you, the space, the room, and with others. Next and at the same time, check in with your self and what is occurring for you in terms of your thoughts, emotions, mood and physiological sensations. Reflect on what you are learning in the moment that will guide your response.

There is much more to us than what others perceive. About 90% of who we are and what we experience is going on under the surface inside us. This is shown visually in the diagram:

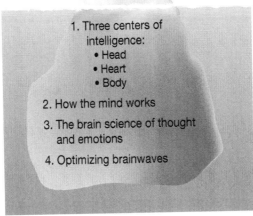

Above the waterline are external experiences (10%)

Behaviors

Below the waterline are internal experiences (90%)

1. Three centers of intelligence:
   • Head
   • Heart
   • Body
2. How the mind works
3. The brain science of thought and emotions
4. Optimizing brainwaves

To cultivate awareness, it is important to understand what is going on for you internally—specifically the following four points:

1. The three sources of intelligence
2. How the mind works
3. The brain science of emotions and thought
4. Brainwaves and authenticity

1. THE THREE SOURCES OF INTELLIGENCE

In order to cultivate awareness, it is helpful to understand that there are three sources of intelligence that can inform your decision-making and behaviours. They include the head (thoughts and beliefs), heart (emotions) and body (sensing and intuition).

Some leaders focus largely on the thinking mind, ignoring their emotions and overriding the sensations of the body—particularly when the inner sensations are signaling that it is time to take a rest. Think of a day when you forgot to eat lunch or take a break, or when you wore shoes that were uncomfortable and you didn't notice how sore your feet and back were until you were back home for the day.

Having more complete information for leading effectively means understanding each of the three centers of intelligence and considering them in more of your decisions and interactions each day.

The following description of each aspect of intelligence is taken directly from the book by Don Richard Riso and Russ Hudson called *The Wisdom of the Enneagram*. While the authors describe each in the context of spiritual and personal development, the Enneagram[22] is becoming more widely known as helpful for leadership development as well. Try substituting the word "leadership" in for "spiritual" when reading the following descriptions:

The Head center of intelligence:

The quiet mind is the source of inner guidance that gives us the ability to perceive reality exactly as it is. It allows us to be receptive to an inner knowing that can guide our actions. Just as we are seldom fully in our bodies or in our hearts, we seldom have access to the quiet, spacious quality of the mind. Quite the contrary, for most of us, the mind is an inner chatterbox, which is why people spend years in monasteries or in retreats trying to quiet their restless minds.[23]

The Heart center of intelligence:

At the deepest level, your heart qualities are the source of your identity. When your heart opens, you know who you are, and that "who you are" has nothing to do with what people think of you and nothing to do with your past history. You have a particular quality, a flavor, something that is unique and intimately you. It is through the heart that we recognize and appreciate our true nature.[24]

The Body center of intelligence:

The body plays a crucial role in all forms of genuine spiritual work, because bringing awareness back to the body anchors the quality of presence. The reason is…while our minds and feelings

---

22   For an overview of the Enneagram Personality System, see Step #1 of the Authentic You™ Personal Planning System – Articulate your Authentic Self, on page ??.

23   Riso and Hudson, The Wisdom of the Enneagram, p 58.

24   Ibid, p 55.

can wander to the past or the future, our body can only exist here and now, in the present moment. This is one of the fundamental reasons why virtually all meaningful spiritual work begins with coming back to the body and becoming more grounded in it. The instincts of the body are the most powerful energies that we have to work with. Any real transformation must involve them [...][25]

You will notice that one of these centers of intelligence is your dominant one. It is helpful to develop awareness of, and to learn to listen to, the guidance of the other two as well.

Alignment of all three centers is important for authentic leaders. It includes objectively choosing the thoughts to listen to, while feeling emotions that are arising and discerning whether they are accurate, particularly in the context of fight-or-flight, and experiencing the physiological sensations that occur, all at the same time. By pairing this with your personal clarity, you have a strong inner guidance system for making choices about your decisions and behaviours.

2. HOW THE MIND WORKS

When you practice awareness, you focus on paying attention to, and understanding how the mind works. By developing your ability to be aware you will be able to lead more objectively as you will not be controlled by your mind. Can you imagine the sense of freedom and relief when you are able to choose a more effective thought and response in the moment, at will?

Your interpretation of every situation is largely based on the experiences you have had in the past, some of which are still applicable, and some of which may be distorting what you think and how you behave. The mind works in mysterious ways and a detailed review is far beyond what is needed as context for this book. It is helpful, though, to understand a few key points as context for developing your practice of awareness.

The main concept to consider is that the mind behaves in certain ways that are consistent across people and cultures. Eckhart Tolle describes these mind states as "conditioned by the past,"[26] and include both *process* (Tolle calls it "structure") and *content*.

---

25   Ibid, p 51.

26   Eckhart Tolle, *A New Earth—Awaken to your Life's Purpose* (New York: Penguin Group, 2005), p 60.

Everyone's mind works according to certain processes that generating specific types of thoughts. Underneath the process there is the mind's content—personality and Authentic Self—which are as unique to each individual as the distinct genetics, influences, and environments that helped to form each person.

Process

The mind is continuously active and the processes it undertakes include—and are not limited to—the following[27]: identification with personality (thinking this is all of who you are and that you cannot change), controlling (yourself or others), longing (for something or someone), wanting (something or someone), identification with objects (in order to feel value or superiority), blaming (others or circumstances), and comparing (yourself to others). These processes are consistent across individuals and cultures.

By developing awareness, you can learn how to recognize these processes and learn to make different choices when they have become unhelpful and show up in their extreme form.

Example: New managers who compare themselves to those who are much more seasoned may have unrealistic expectations of their abilities to manage complex issues that require years of experience. As a result they may not ask for help or involve others in decision making resulting in a public relations and business risk.

When new managers becomes aware of their habits, they can override this mental process and choose a more effective response. They will then have a more realistic and compassionate perspective of their selves and will ask for assistance or work with others given their evolved expectations.

Constant comparing, where unwarranted, can create unhelpful levels of stress and ineffective behaviours. Awareness and self-management (managing the internal experiences for more effective external ones) can mitigate this process, leading to a greater capacity for authenticity, and action that serves all involved.

---

27   Ibid, p 59, 60.

Content

While the *processes* of the mind are consistent across individuals, the *content* is unique to each.

Content—the topics that the mind dwells on, come from 1) the personality (what Tolle calls "ego"): messages each individual has stored on their inner "tapes" that play over and over in their mind, providing guidance and perspective in every moment; as well as 2) the Authentic Self: the more pure being that each of us is born with.

Content evolves based on who you are at birth as well as your experiences as a child, and your upbringing, influences and culture.

"Unless you know the basic mechanics behind the workings of the ego, you won't recognize it, and it will trick you into identifying with it again and again. This means it takes you over, an imposter pretending to be you."[28]

"The stronger the ego, the stronger the sense of separateness between people. The only actions that do not cause opposing reactions are those that are aimed at the good of all. They are inclusive, not exclusive. They join; they don't separate. They are not for "my" country but for all of humanity, not for "my" religion but for the emergence of consciousness in all human beings, not for "my" species but for all sentient beings and all of nature".[29]

The following is an example of how the mind works within leaders in organizations:

Example: George, a senior leader within a large organization, leads a team for new business development. He has been told that his behaviour of blaming other departments when problems arise, will hold him back if he wants to move to the next level of his career. George believes that the other departments made the mistakes and they should be held accountable.

---

28   Tolle, Eckhart, *A New Earth—Awakening to Your Life's Purpose - 52 Inspirational Cards.* New World Library Namaste Publishing.

29   Tolle, *A New Earth* (book), p 60.

*The **process** at work in the mind is blaming. The **content** is the belief that he can keep the spotlight off himself by blaming the other departments when things go wrong.*

George's unhelpful behaviour continues until he receives feedback from his manager. He experiences the cognitive dissonance that occurs when he realizes who he is being is not the same as what he believed to be true about himself. George realizes he must do something and he enrolls a coach to provide targeted support.

He develops awareness and begins to see the process of blaming for what it is—the way the mind works. He experiences an awakening as he sees, for the first time in his life, that the biased mind can provide incorrect guidance at times—and he can learn to let it go. George can also see the content of his mind—the aspect of personality that no longer serves him—and can override it. He can see that his perceptions were based on old ideas of inferiority. By remembering his Authentic Self, and his innate worth, and by respecting those around him, he can now take personal responsibility for his part in the problem, as well as share the credit for the accomplishments.

When he is at his best, in addition to being an excellent businessperson, George is generous, kind and empathetic. When he remembers this then he begins to live authentically in more and more situations. George begins to make choices as an emotionally and socially mature adult, rather than basing them on beliefs he learned as—and that may have been more appropriate for—a child or young adult.

George's ability to be authentic has a ripple effect on others around him. People who work for him become drawn to his calm demeanor, consistency, and caring style. They in turn feel comfortable to be authentic when interacting with him—particularly when they want to disagree, challenge his assumptions, and/or need to have difficult conversations.

George learns to take on a positive outlook. With each conscious choice he makes, he begins to pay attention to how life is unfold-

ing for him. In what may be the first time in his life, he is leading in a way that is congruent with what is truly important to him.

George takes the time to renew his personal clarity. He reflects on and articulates his purpose, values, leadership principles and life vision. This creates an awakening that opens up different possibilities for him. He now has new guideposts for leading, and he has a deeper understanding of the right thing to do from a business and an ethical perspective.

3. THE BRAIN SCIENCE OF EMOTIONS AND THOUGHT[30]

Volumes have been written on the subject of the science of the mind. For the purposes of this book it is helpful to understand it at an introductory level, and in the context of how it supports Authentic Leadership.

First, let's look at the emotional and rational parts of the brain and how they work together; and second, we'll discuss brainwaves and how the right combination of brainwaves can support authenticity through a calm, alert mind.

The Parts of the Brain

As a result of evolution, the brain is composed of three separate parts (see diagram below). First there is the reptilian brain, which is the oldest part. It developed when it was important to assess whether a situation meant, "eat or be eaten." It is responsible for assessing risk, and as a result it reacts the quickest of the three. The second part—the limbic system—appeared first in mammals and acts as the emotional centre. The third part to evolve was the prefrontal area, or the neocortex, which governs rational thought. [31]

---

30   Appreciations to my team members at ViRTUS (www.virtusinc.com), who inspired me to add the brain science to this book.

31   *The Evolutionary Layers of the Human Brain,* http://thebrain.mcgill.ca/flash/d/d_05/d_05_cr/d_05_cr_her/d_05_cr_her.html, 2012.

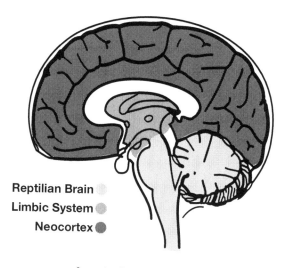

Reptilian Brain
Limbic System
Neocortex

Source: http://tinyurl.com/c9stkuv

Within the limbic system is the amygdala, a structure of the emotional centre, which is responsible for assessing situations you encounter for whether they are safe or a risk. It uses past experiences to assess the level of risk, which may or may not be accurate in the current situation. If the amygdala senses risk, the sympathetic nervous system takes over and your mind and body will experience "flight, fight or freeze." Your thinking mind has been taken over by the emotional centre.

"This arrangement worked well during the last 100 million or so years of evolution. Fear guided early mammals through the real dangers of predators; anger mobilized a mother to fight to protect her young. And social emotions such as jealousy, pride, contempt, and affection all played a role in the family politics of primate groups— just as they do in the underworld of organizational life today.

While emotions have guided human survival through evolution, a neural dilemma for leadership has emerged in the last 10,000 years or so. In today's advanced civilization, we face complex social realities (say, the sense someone isn't treating us fairly) with a brain designed for surviving physical emergencies. And so we can find ourselves hijacked—swept away by anxiety or anger better suited for handling bodily threats than the subtleties of office

50

politics. (Just who the hell does this guy think he is! I'm so mad I could punch him.)"[32]

When in fight or flight, your body produces adrenaline as well as the stress hormone cortisol. You experience anxiousness and your ability to be creative and to make decisions is reduced. In addition, if you are in this state for long periods of time (let's say a successful career of 15—35 years), your body becomes used to being stressed and there can be long-term health implications such as elevated cortisol levels and/or adrenal fatigue.

Adrenal fatigue, which Dr. James Wilson describes as "The 21st Century Stress Syndrome,"[33] is another name for burnout. It occurs when the body is overloaded with stress and a fast-paced lifestyle for a period of years, and when the immune system simply cannot keep up. It impacts resiliency and effectiveness as a leader, and over time can lead to other serious health issues. It also impacts authenticity, as stress means that you are more likely to regress to automatic patterns of thought and behaviour when you don't have the energy to choose to be authentic.

When you are relaxed, alternatively, the prefrontal area of the brain can veto an unhelpful emotional impulse. The relaxation response supports production of the neural transmitter dopamine, which improves your effectiveness both interpersonally, as well as in your ability to learn and make decisions.

Authentic leaders are able to self-manage in the moment when the emotional part of the brain incorrectly identifies risk and sends them into fight or flight. They can identify what is occurring more objectively and can override their emotions to choose a more appropriate response.

Brainwaves and authenticity

Brainwaves are another fascinating topic related to the science of the mind. They provide an important link between mainstream business, eastern philosophies and meditation (or mindfulness).

Anna Wise provides a useful review of brainwaves in her book *The High-Performance Mind—Mastering Brainwaves for Insight, Healing, and*

---

32   Daniel Goleman, *Primal Leadership—Learning to Lead with Emotional Intelligence* (Boston: Harvard Business School Press, 2002), p 28.

33   Dr. James Wilson, N.D., D.C., Ph.D., *Adrenal Fatigue – The 21st Century Stress Syndrome.* 13th printing. (Petaluma, CA: Smart Publications, 2009), p 11.

Creativity.[34] Wise introduces the idea that you can, at will, create the conditions for the optimal combination of brainwave functioning in order to experience the high-performance or "awakened" mind.

There are 4 different kinds of brainwaves: beta, alpha, theta and delta. These are electrical impulses that are occurring all the time. During day-to-day normal activities, you will experience an abundance of Beta brainwaves called splayed beta. These can, however, cause challenges when you experience too much mental functioning, worry, a sense of anxiousness and/or feeling scattered.

> "Many people can successfully operate out in the world producing only, or at least primarily, this brainwave pattern. Apart from being a somewhat uncomfortable mental state, splayed beta is not a fully conscious state, either. How interesting that the conscious mind—beta waves—can be thought of as not conscious. This is what Gurdjieff has called "waking sleep." In pure beta we are not awake to ourselves. We are not awake to our innermost being, our subconscious, our unconscious, our intuition, our deeper sense of spirituality, and our latent creativity and potential. This is what the awakened mind is about."[35]

Alpha is experienced when you are in a relaxed, alert, calm state. Theta is experienced during peak experiences when there is something locked in the brain and you can almost access it from your unconsciousness; and Delta is experienced as a personal sense of radar, and is important to intuition and empathy.

In the corporate world, you may have learned to overuse your beta brainwaves as these are the ones produced when you are thinking, making decisions and are multi-tasking. Think of times during your day when you are feeling scattered and anxious or your brain feels full. It is an overabundance of beta brainwaves that is at play.

What can be helpful is to exercise the brain through meditation and visualization (think of going to the gym for your mind) to learn to master cultivating the optimal combination of brainwaves at any time. Mindfulness or meditation practices—particularly those that use as many of the five senses as possible—are essential to support awareness and self-managing

---

34   Wise, *The High-Performance Mind,* p 1 .

35   Ibid, p 13-14.

(which will be introduced in the next chapter) – two foundational competencies of an authentic leader.

Authentic leaders are able to create the conditions for the optimal amounts of each brainwave, depending on the situation they are in. By having the right amount of beta (i.e. thinking), while accessing alpha, theta and delta brainwaves, you can create the conditions for brain functioning for creativity, insight and maintaining perspective:

> "When you produce all of these frequencies together in the right proportion and relationship with one another, you experience the intuitive, empathetic radar of the delta waves; the creative inspiration, personal insight, and spiritual awareness of the theta waves; the bridging capacity and relaxed, detached, awareness of the alpha waves; and the ability of the beta waves to consciously process thought, all at the same time!".[36]

They are also able to practice resting for resiliency during their busiest days—days which may include back-to-back meetings, hundreds of emails, voicemails and "tweets"—through short, meditation practices in between tasks.

The brainwave pattern of a high-performance mind supports authentic leaders as they can then maintain perspective and have the capacity to check in with their inner guidance for their choices and behaviours.

SUMMARY

Awareness includes two aspects—personal clarity (recognizing who you are when at your best and what is important to you in your leadership and life), as well as awareness on a day-to-day basis. Personal clarity includes understanding and articulating your Authentic Self, values, purpose, leadership principles, life vision, work-life balance, goals or intentions and inner development plan. The day-to-day evolving awareness includes a practice of checking in with yourself on an ongoing basis—both internally and externally as well as your impact on others. As context, it is helpful to understand the 3 centres of intelligence, how your mind works—both process and content— as well as a bit about the science of emotions, thought and brainwaves so you can learn to create the optimal conditions for practicing being authentic.

---

36   Ibid, p 10.

CHAPTER SIX:
ACTION

*What occurs for you externally is just the tip of the iceberg—
the really exciting experiences are those that occur
internally, below the surface of the water.*

Once you have experienced an awakening, and you are ready to listen to it, your awareness will grow. You will experience the inner tension that arises with cognitive dissonance and you will need to do something in order to reduce your feelings of discomfort. Action must be taken.

Actions are the steps that you take both internally and externally. By managing the former, you will be more effective at the latter.

Authentic leaders are aware that action occurs in two realms: first internally, and second externally. The iceberg image illustrates how a very small percentage of ourselves is composed of our external experiences.

First let's dive in to what occurs below the surface in the inner realm and how to self-manage, and then we'll look at three behaviours that are helpful to develop to support authenticity.

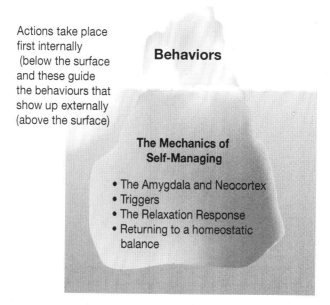

Actions take place first internally (below the surface and these guide the behaviours that show up externally (above the surface)

Behaviors

The Mechanics of Self-Managing

- The Amygdala and Neocortex
- Triggers
- The Relaxation Response
- Returning to a homeostatic balance

INTERNAL ACTION—SELF-MANAGING

Authentic leaders know that action takes place first internally and then externally.

The action that will first take place *internally* is self-managing. You will learn to choose which thoughts you pay attention to among the endless stream that occur each day. You will also learn to self-manage (or self-regulate) to override unhelpful, habitual thoughts, emotions and sensations, in the moment.

Note: your internal experiences may go largely unnoticed by others unless you are transparent and tell them what is occurring for you. They may however, notice a confusing incongruence at times between what you are saying and what they are sensing is occurring for you.

THE MECHANICS OF SELF-MANAGING

Self-managing is the ability to notice when you are triggered by a situation or person, to notice the impacts on the other person, and to stay aware and effective, as it is occurring.

Although you are triggered, you remain objective and present to how your mind is working throughout the interaction and what is occurring physiologically as you experience stress. At an advanced level, you are able to choose an appropriate behaviour in the moment, and to notice how the uncomfortable feelings dissipate as a state of relative relaxation returns.

ARC OF INTENSE ENERGY

Self-managing through the arc of intense energy is an advanced ability found in emotionally intelligent and authentic individuals and takes time and extensive practice to master.

The arc of intense energy (shown in the diagram below) is a mental model for thinking about what occurs as you self-manage. It can be difficult to stay present in each moment and particularly in uncomfortable situations. Your emotions and sensations may feel like a wave of intense energy that builds, peaks and then eventually dissipates—this experience is depicted as an arc.

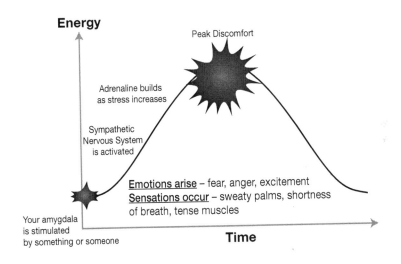

In the diagram, you will see two axes—the horizontal axis represents time in seconds as this all occurs very quickly. The vertical axis shows the intensity of energy that builds and dissipates in the body after you are triggered—caught off-guard or startled by something or someone.

The peak of the arc is a heightened level of discomfort as opposed to peak performance. This is an important distinction.

Once you are caught off guard by, for example, a comment someone makes about a problem with a product you have just produced, your mind goes into action and interprets the situation. Your body goes into a fight-or-flight like state as your brain sends a message of a threat, and your sympathetic nervous system kicks in. Your breathing becomes shallow, your palms sweat and your ability to interact effectively and make decisions declines.

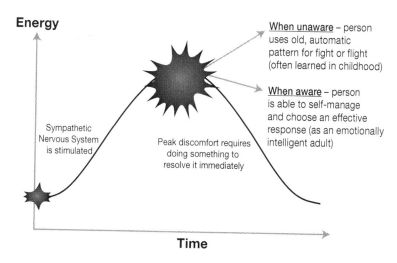

Energy

When unaware – person uses old, automatic pattern for fight or flight (often learned in childhood)

When aware – person is able to self-manage and choose an effective response (as an emotionally intelligent adult)

Sympathetic Nervous System is stimulated

Peak discomfort requires doing something to resolve it immediately

Time

Self-managing requires the ability to be aware of both the inner experience and how it is impacting your external one—your behaviours, at the same time as noticing your impact on others. As you develop this simultaneous awareness, internally you may begin to notice the emotions that are arising, the sensations as you enter fight, flight or freeze responses, and the energy intensifying in your body.

When you are unaware, conversely, at the peak of the arc where the energy is most intense, you with think and behave using old, automatic patterns of reacting. These behaviours may be appropriate, or they may be self-limiting and unhelpful. They are based on the unique content of your personality. For example, one person's pattern may be to get defensive and yell; another's may be to shut down and withdraw; yet another's may be to get confused and cry. None of which may be helpful in the situation.

Self-managing also requires the ability to intentionally bring about the relaxation response.[37]

---

37   Ibid, p 27.

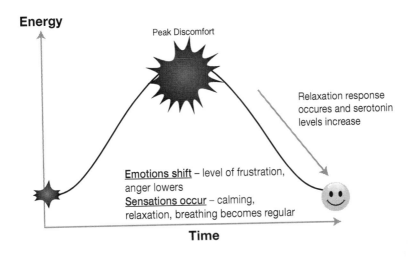

Energy

Peak Discomfort

Relaxation response
occures and serotonin
levels increase

<u>Emotions shift</u> – level of frustration,
anger lowers
<u>Sensations occur</u> – calming,
relaxation, breathing becomes regular

Time

Relaxation requires being able to focus your attention on your breath and to change it from shallow to a deep and consistent level of breathing. As you do this it provides oxygen for the brain as well as a distraction for the mind for just long enough to regain your composure and perspective.

Being able to relax the body through focused deep breathing is key to effective brain functioning. As you learn to manage your brainwaves, you will be able to reduce the amount of beta—the brainwaves that kick in when the emotional centre of the brain has hijacked a situation and you are in full on fight, flight or freeze. As you return to a calmer state, you will access the alpha brainwaves required for maintaining perspective and choosing a different response.

This ability can be developed through a simple sitting practice, a guided meditation or yoga breathing. The more you practice, the more you build your capacity to quickly refocus the mind in order to choose thoughts and behaviours more aligned with your Authentic Self.

As you practice deep breathing you can also learn to recognize emotions as they arise, to hear the guidance from the heart centre of intelligence, as well as to listen to your body centre and intuition.

You will also learn to check objectively whether it is your Authentic Self shining through to guide you, or unhelpful aspects of your personality that are showing up. Remember the switch—personality or Authentic Self. You get to choose in each moment, which one you will align your behaviours with.

When you are able to stay alert and aware, you can objectively choose the behaviour that is aligned with who you are, and that will be the most effective in the current situation.

"In that moment of awareness, we may realize that we do not really want to do the questionable behaviour that only seconds before we were so invested in. We may also see a deeper truth about our situation—for instance, that the "important point" we were so eager to make was really only an attempt to justify ourselves, or worse, a covert attempt to get back at someone."[38]

Your choice of behaviour may range from doing nothing in the moment (for example, you are in a group setting and you would prefer to give the person feedback in private) to setting a clear boundary for the team and refocusing the conversation. Or you may choose to disagree and point out a misalignment with organizational values and direction.

Being authentic doesn't mean being soft—it means being mature and clear and able to lead in a way that is aligned with your Personal or Inner Clarity, strong ethics, and Authentic Self.

SHIFTING PERSPECTIVE

Self-managing may require a shift in your perspective.

Shifting perspective, or reframing, means that you open to new possibilities for how to think about a topic, situation or person. Think of a beautiful piece of art and how different it will look during the day with natural light, in the evening with a spotlight pointed directly at it, or when viewed by an art expert versus a person who is not interested in art. Each person perceives the painting differently. Sometimes it helps to shift the way you think about something in order to see it in a new, more effective way.

The way you think about things is based on your experience to this point in your life, and it may need to shift in order for you to move to the next stage in your leadership.

Example: Margaret is a leader of a small public relations firm. She has worked there for 15 years and resists technology. She believes that social networking on the company computers will

---

38   Riso and Hudson, *The Wisdom of the Enneagram*, p 37.

mean that employees will take advantage of their time at work to spend more time than is appropriate socializing with friends and family. This resistance is based on a fear of technology and a lack of understanding of the opportunities it offers.

Margaret's resistance may be getting in the way of huge opportunities for reaching potential clients, for working effectively with employees who are well versed in social technologies such as Google +, Linked In, Twitter and Facebook, and for providing public relation solutions for existing clients.

A peer gives Margaret feedback about her resistance, and at first she finds it hard to hear.

Then she begins to talk to others who have a passion for technology and she begins to see it in a different way—she shifts her perspective. She begins to try out social networking technologies. She attends courses to understand the potential for businesses, and she also looks at how she thinks about her employees.

When she realizes she has a trust issue and needs to practice trusting others, she begins to interact with them in new ways. She begins to delegate more to a small team who are interested in social technology. They undertake a project to look at how it can serve the business and its clients.

Margaret sets up a strategy session to change how the business uses social networking and becomes a leader in the public relations field in this area.

Once you have shifted your perspective, you can begin to do something differently—in a new, more effective way.

There are countless times throughout each day—at work and outside of work—when it is of benefit to slow down, become very intentional about how you are interacting with yourself and others, and shift your perspective through self-management.

SELF-MANAGING AND BEING PRESENT

Multi-tasking—where attention is split between several thoughts such as the next thing that needs to be completed, or another project that is also important—is in vogue as an essential competency for good leaders. It can, however, be distracting and take away from authenticity. When your attention is scattered, it can mean the experience that is occurring is largely ignored. This diminishes the quality of the interaction. When the interaction is with an employee, peer, or client, this can weaken the relationship and reduce the intended result as well.

Practicing being present (letting go of all other things to focus completely on the person or task in this moment) supports focus, clarity and quality of interactions—essential for effective social skills and development of long-term, trust-based relationships. While this is important for face-to-face interactions, it is even more essential for situations when verbal cues are not present—on the phone and other forms of social networking and technology such as email and texting, in which interactions are in writing.

Once you are aware of the arc of intense energy, you can practice (sometimes moment by moment, depending on the day) self-managing to centre or relax into the present. Your awareness may include noticing the endless stream of thoughts that pass through your mind, and the emotions and physiological sensations that occur. You can observe them objectively, and let them go in order to focus on the task or person in front of you.

Awareness might also include letting go of the inner critic or the negative voices that play out in your mind and that can guide your life and your leadership in ways that are not helpful. You may also become aware of and less attached to the processes of the mind. These may include noticing wanting to be like someone you know who is more successful than you or in a position that you covet, or identifying with objects to increase a sense of your personal worth (gotta have that $2500 purse), and letting these thoughts go in order to stay present to the moment that is now.

In the book Slowing Down to the Speed of Life, Carlson and Bailey introduce two distinct modes of thinking[39] —first is the frantic, analytical, computer-like mode; and second is creative, free-flow. If you think of a child and how they can play for hours, or a time when you were doing

---

39   Richard Carlson and Joseph Bailey, *Slowing down to the Speed of Life—How to create a more peaceful, simpler life from the inside out* (New York: HarperCollins Books, 1997), pp. 11 - 15.

something you love and all of the sudden it was several hours later—this is creative free-flow. It is another way to describe being present and is essential for creativity and living authentically. It also requires less energy as you effortlessly live in the moment.

As you grow into adulthood you become socialized to doing what is valued—multi-tasking, focusing on constantly increasing your productivity, getting more done with less, adding technology into the mix so you can get even more done—and you become used to the frantic, busy, computer-like mode of thinking.

For effective leadership and for your well-being you need to "remember" the creative free-flow and build your capacity to be choiceful about when you step into the "busy-ness" and to be able to pull out and live in the second mode, more of the time.

SELF-MANAGING AND THE INNER CRITIC[40]

Imagine what it would be like if you talked to yourself like you talked to your best friend? With kindness, empathy and understanding.

This is possible, more of the time, as you learn to manage your inner critic (the negative voice, or unhelpful aspect of your personality, that can be controlling how you lead and live your life).

There are three things to consider about the inner critic: first, it will always be there and as you become aware of it, it may become even louder; second, it is possible to shift how you experience the inner critic when it comes up; and third, compassion—both for yourself and for others—is the gateway.

The inner critics shows up as an often mean-spirited, critical thought, or sensation that lasts just a few seconds—or longer if you obsess about or replay it.

In its basic form it is the internalization of the messages you received as a child and young adult, from others around you who influenced you at that time.

When others reacted to your way of being, and you felt humiliated or intimidated by them, you learned that it would be less painful to criticize yourself first than to experience it through them. So you internalized the inner critic and it became the standard-setter and judgmental voice that guides your life.

---

40   For resources and support for understanding and managing your Inner Critic, see www.leadauthentic.com

You can learn to self-manage when it arises, and to step into your Authentic Self more of the time in spite of it. This may include learning to see it for what it is in its fleeting form. To keep it in perspective, laugh at it at times, scream at it at times (in your head) and practice letting it go. You will notice that its volume gets louder or softer depending on how well you are, your current level of resiliency, and whether you have been consistent with your personal self-care regimen. For some, your inner critic may be so loud that it may seem that there isn't just one—there is a committee of them, or a board of directors.

Imagine how much energy you have spent listening to, and being impacted by the inner critic to this point. Imagine also, what it will be like as you are able to let it go and relax into being your Authentic Self. Learning to have empathy or compassion for yourself and others is very helpful. So too is spending time with your community of support to discuss, learn, and share experiences and insights that you can then incorporate into your life.

FOUR COMMON SITUATIONS IN WHICH SELF-MANAGING IS HELPFUL

The following are common situations in a corporate setting in which self-managing is most helpful. These are situations that are:

* Uncomfortable or difficult
* Culturally new
* Generationally different
* Creatively new

Each one provides an opportunity to practice awareness and self-managing for more effective interactions and outcomes.

Uncomfortable or Difficult situations

As a leader you will encounter potentially uncomfortable or difficult situations each day. These can range from having a conversation with an employee with whom there is a performance issue; to meeting with the Board to explain a costly decision you, as an Executive, made; to meeting with a customer who has been neglected and whose concern has fallen through the cracks, to providing feedback to a peer whose behaviour is out of alignment with the company and your personal values.

When you encounter an uncomfortable or difficult situation, you can either see it as something to avoid at all costs, or as an opportunity that will help you to strengthen and grow.

Many times, if a leader is lacking the skill or confidence to have difficult conversations, the situations are either deferred indefinitely or they are dealt with after it is too late to remedy them simply and effectively.

In his book *A Path with Heart*, Jack Kornfield shares a story about a potentially difficult situation involving a poisonous tree and how three groups of passersby chose to see it with distinctly different lenses.[41] While Kornfield refers to development on a spiritual path, it is similar to the leadership path of a corporate leader who continuously learns, shifts perspective, and gains wisdom in order to act in increasingly authentic ways:

> On first discovering a poisoned tree, some people see only its danger. Their immediate reaction is, "Let's cut this down before we are hurt. Let's cut it down before anyone else eats of the poisoned fruit." This resembles our initial response to the difficulties that arise in our lives, when we encounter aggression, compulsion, greed, or fear, when we are faced with stress, loss, conflict, depression, or sorrow in ourselves and others. Our initial response is to avoid them, saying, "These poisons afflict us. Let us uproot them; let us be rid of them. Let us cut them down."

> Other people, who have journeyed further along the spiritual path, discover this poisoned tree and do not meet it with aversion. They have realized that to open to life requires a deep and heartfelt compassion for all that is around us. Knowing the poisoned tree is somehow a part of us, they say, "Let us not cut it down. Instead, let's have compassion for the tree as well." So out of kindness they build a fence around the tree so that others may not be poisoned and the tree may also have its life. This second approach shows a profound shift of relationship from judgment and fear to compassion.

> A third type of person, who has traveled yet deeper in spiritual life, sees this same tree. This person, who has gained much vision, looks and says, "Oh, a poisoned tree. Perfect! Just what I was looking for." This individual picks the poisoned fruit, investigates its properties, mixes it with other ingredients, and uses the

---

41   Jack Kornfield, *A Path With Heart—A Guide through the Perils and Promises of Spiritual Life* (New York: Bantam Books, 1993), p 78.

poison as a great medicine to heal the sick and transform the ills of the world. Through respect and understanding, this person sees in a way opposite to most people and finds value in most difficult circumstances.....

In each an every aspect of life, the chance to turn the straw we find into gold is there in our hearts. All that is asked is our respectful attention, our willingness to learn from difficulty. Instead of fighting, when we see with eyes of wisdom, difficulties can become our good fortune.[42]

Culturally new

Each day you may meet people of different cultural backgrounds to your own and not even know it. Or maybe you do and yet you may be less aware of their cultural context in your interactions.

Authenticity means having the ability to empathize with another person and to be aware that you may not know what is going on for them in this moment, on this day in their lives. They could have a way of thinking about and building relationships and doing business that differs from yours. It is your responsibility to take the time, as well as have the sincere interest, to understand how they want to be in relationship with you.

Think of it as practicing "other-centred" relationship building where you may have no idea of the implications of your tone, body language, beliefs, dress, or manner. And so each interaction needs to be thoughtful and intentional.

The practice for leaders is to be aware and authentic, rather than unaware and assuming.

Generationally different

People of different generations and ages have grown up with influences, which will have very different impacts on their values, leadership principles and how they choose to live their lives. A person who grew up with technology as a given, from an early age, may have a different worldview and experience of life than a person who grew up in the 60's rock and roll scene, or a person who participated in the Second World War or grew up in the depression.

When in doubt check it out—take the time to ask.

---

42   Ibid.

Rather than judging people for their differences, authentic leaders notice their judgments as they arise; they then park them and stay open and curious in order to respectfully engage with the other person. This emphasizes the importance of practicing "other-centred" relationship building in which you apply the 5th Habit of Stephen Covey's *Seven Habits of Highly Effective People*: "Seek first to understand before being understood."[43]

Listening with a willingness to be influenced[44] can help build relationships in any interaction, particularly with people of a different generation. Who knows—if you are open to your assumptions being challenged, you may learn something new that will shift the way you think for the rest of your life.

Creatively new

Innovation and creativity are corporate assets. The leaders' job is to provide the conditions for employees to feel inspired to create.

Product and service solutions are being developed daily by marketing and development teams globally. The leader who inspires this and ensures the employees have the resiliency, space, time and motivation to be innovative, has the golden egg for profitable growth. Authentic leaders hire and seek out employees who will challenge their assumptions and push the boundaries (within appropriate limits) in order to discover the next generation of customer solutions.

To maintain an open mind while your assumptions and beliefs are being challenged, it can be helpful to be able to self-manage. This allows your impact on the employee to be an inspiring one, rather than one that creates fear and humiliation, shutting them down, and stifling creativity permanently.

Self-managing is also essential for pulling out of multi-tasking mode to enter the creative space where relaxation and open-mindedness is crucial; as well as for letting go of limiting beliefs and behaviours such as shutting down others during brainstorming sessions ("we've done it before so it won't work now')—again stifling creativity.

In addition to the above four situations, self-managing can be helpful for everything from letting go of unhelpful behaviours with significant others at home, to how you interact with your children and yourself. It

43   Stephen Covey, 5th Habit, *Seven Habits of Highly Effective People*, https://www.stephencovey.com/7habits/7habits-habit5.php

44   Source: Integral Coaching Program, New Ventures West.

improves interpersonal skills in general and is foundational for emotional and social intelligence.

EXTERNAL ACTION—BEHAVIOUR

Once you are aware of your thoughts and what else is occurring *internally*, you will be able to choose a more effective behaviour for your *external* experiences. Rather than accepting a default reaction, you can build capacity for the prefrontal area of your brain to override an emotional impulse and choose a response that is different from how you have behaved in the past.

Each time you choose to behave in a way that is congruent with your values, purpose, and leadership principles, you make a course correction on your journey to being authentic. You adjust or re-align your life and your leadership more closely to your Authentic Self, and you grow as a person. Your brain function improves as well, as the emotional and rational centres learn to work more effectively together.

Example: After you become aware of the impact your personality is having on your relationships, you begin to notice your thoughts and judgments when interacting with others. You notice your impatience arising and your assumption that these people are insufficient somehow, and that they are weak and they "just don't get it".

In response, you practice self-managing—you slow down your breathing. You relax and practice empathy. You choose to override your impatience and ask the other person how their day is going.

You notice how you begin to feel more patience and compassion for them as they share, for example, that they have had not slept properly for six months since their new child was born. You may have had no idea about their personal situation, and yet you worked with them most of the days over that time.

When you change, the other person will notice this and may regain trust as she/he experiences you differently and more consistently over time.

Other people can then relax around you as they can feel that you care. They can then be more effective in their work.

As you learn to self-manage, people will become more engaged with you, particularly if you share with them what aspect of your personality you are currently working on in your effort to become authentic.

BEHAVIOURS THAT SUPPORT AUTHENTICITY

There are the three foundational behaviours that support authenticity. By practicing these on an ongoing basis, you will have more capacity to stand in your truth and to be authentic in the moment. These practices provide a starting point for every leader who chooses to live aligned with their Authentic Self. They include:

1. Self-Care—nutrition, exercise, mindfulness, timeout to "unplug" (resiliency for perspective)
2. Saying no and setting boundaries (clarity in the moment)
3. Having difficult conversations and managing conflict (for exceptional social skills)

1. Self-Care

Practicing self-care for wellness and work-life balance is an essential support for authenticity, and to live from a place of calm and inner clarity.

Self-care includes having a personal philosophy about a holistic approach to wellness. It includes understanding what is the customized approach to nutrition that will support you to be the best you can be—to know what foods and supplements build your energy as opposed to draining it. It also includes exercises, mindfulness practices and scheduling "time outs" in order to disconnect from the day-to-day and to return to a sense of calm through holidays, retreats and time for self-reflection.

Personal wellness supports being authentic in a number of ways—when you are well rested, get the right amount of exercise, and have nutritional practices that optimizes your health, energy and clarity of mind, you have more capacity to do the following:

- Maintain a sense of calm in what others would experience as incredibly intense and uncomfortable situations,
- Maintain a sense of perspective in situations where in the past you may have been "thrown" and went immediately into an old, unhelpful, automatic pattern,

- Stay present to the discomfort of emotions that arise, in order to set a boundary, say no where you need to, let go of an old habit (or addiction) that may be getting in the way of your being the best you can be,
- See your inner critic for what it is—just an unhelpful thought that can be let go of in order to choose a more mature, objective response,
- Ensure that your foundation outside of work is in place—i.e. family commitments are in place—to support effectiveness at work and visa versa,
- Have more fun while you get things accomplished, and laugh at yourself rather than taking things personally when they don't always go your way, and
- Other things, which you don't even know about yet, as you are this far on your journey and they have yet to arise.

2. Learn to say no and to set boundaries

Can you think of a time when you have said yes to a task or situation and you really wanted to say no? What was it like for you? What was the impact?

Do any of these situations sound familiar? Are you the manager who continues to "do" rather than to delegate to your team members thinking, "It's too much effort to explain all the details, I'll just do that myself." Are you the executive who takes on more groups and more accountabilities rather than being thoughtful about how much will be too much for you— thinking "Of course I can take on that new group with 300 extra people. How will I manage? I'll figure it out." Or are you the leader who books events every night of the week—volunteering, going to school, social evenings for work—and then crashes on the weekend?

There are four things to consider when learning how to say no. First, it can help to understand the interplay between over-functioning and anger. Some people take on too much, consistently, and feel frustrated when others don't. Others are clear about their accountabilities and respect their boundaries for what is too much so won't say yes, at all costs.

Second, slowing and listening to your body, your emotions, and your feelings can support you to know when you are taking on too much. The body provide signals, if you choose to listen to them, that support you to maintain your personal boundaries.

Third, clarifying what's acceptable to you—your values and boundaries—supports you to say no.

And self-compassion is key as you learn a new way. You are in this life for the long term and progress isn't always linear.

Remember than building any new skill will take time and will feel uncomfortable at first. As you build capacity, situations which in the past seemed ominous will have less and less impact on you. As you get used to saying no, you will be able to do it in more situations. You may be.aware of a momentary discomfort as you set a boundary, but soon you will easily accomplish what in the past would have been a difficult conversation.

It becomes your new way, and you have shifted the old.

3. Practice having difficult conversations and managing conflict

Difficult conversations are a "gift" you will be given over and over again in your life. Building your capacity to have these conversation can help you to be authentic as you stand in your truth. It will also help to minimize and manage stress.

Each time you have a conversation that is uncomfortable for you, it is a confidence-building opportunity; you are developing a life-long skill. And with support and practice it becomes less difficult over time.

In addition to having difficult conversations, it is important to learn how to manage conflict. From time to time conflict may arise. When it does, you can learn to see each situation is a crossroads for a relationship.

It can be helpful to understand your current automatic (default) patterns and beliefs for dealing with conflict, and to become aware of what may need to shift in order to improve your effectiveness.

Conflict may arise in different kinds of situations. For some, situations you may be able to avoid conflict in the moment by simply looking at and questioning your interpretation of events. In situations where the other person's behaviour is out of alignment with your values, you may need to set a boundary. And finally, in situations where there is an unworkable incongruence in values, you may need to leave the relationship.

Clearing annoyances as soon as they occur supports minimizing conflict, and the amount of energy you expend on it. When you clear *annoyances* on an ongoing basis, you may avoid potential *big issues* that have, through time, grown out of proportion.

SUMMARY

Authentic leaders know that action takes place first internally, and then externally. Internal action involves the ability to self-manage—maintaining perspective and effectiveness in the wake of the amygdala putting the body into fight, flight or freeze. Managing brainwave activity creates optimal conditions for being authentic as well. Self-managing helps us let go of multitasking in order to be present, let go of the inner critic, and be more effective in other situations as well—difficult or uncomfortable, culturally different, generationally different, and creatively new.

Next, Action takes place externally as leaders are better able to question their automatic reactions and choose a more effective behaviour in the moment. There are three foundational behaviours that, when practiced, cultivate authenticity—self-care for resiliency, saying no and setting boundaries, and having difficult conversations and managing conflict.

CHAPTER SEVEN:
AUTHENTICITY AND EMOTIONAL AND SOCIAL INTELLIGENCE

Authenticity provides the path to
developing emotional and social intelligence.

By adopting the practices outlined within this book, authentic leaders will develop their of emotional and social intelligence.

Emotional and social intelligence is a set of emotional and social skills (that can be learned and improved upon) that support more effective relationships with both yourself and others. They also support having more enjoyable and effective experiences in the world.

Daniel Goleman's Model of emotional and social intelligence[45] includes five hallmarks:

- Self-awareness
- Self-regulation
- Motivation
- Empathy
- Social Skills

Self-awareness (awareness) and self-regulation (self-management) have already been discussed at length and are essential to becoming an authentic leader. They are the basis for emotional and social intelligence and

---

45   Daniel Goleman, "What Makes a Leader?", p 1.

the first two hallmarks of Goleman's model. In addition, personal or inner clarity provides the basis for intrinsic motivation, the third hallmark and is gained by completing the Authentic You™ Personal Planning System. This will be discussed in detail in the next chapter.

Let's touch on the other hallmarks now.

MOTIVATION

Authentic leaders must balance being motivated by deeply held beliefs and personal clarity with the added attraction of external rewards such as incentives and recognition.

Authentic Leadership fosters being intentional about decision making and always checking the internal motivation for the behaviour at hand. For example, if a leader is working with a contractor who, they discover, is acting out of alignment with the values of the company, the leader's personal values, and the laws of the land, they have a choice in how to react. They can do nothing, they can talk to the contractor, they can check with their workplace advisor or code of conduct expert, or the company legal counsel.

The situation may be extremely uncomfortable and the leader may have a pattern of avoiding any interaction that could be confrontational. Authentic leaders, however, have a clear inner guidance system fueled by their personal clarity, and this includes an awareness of a global, ethical context. They will know exactly what to do, even though their mind may want to go to the old pattern of avoiding. Awareness and self-managing will support them through the discomfort, to stay true to their values and to do the right thing.

As a reminder, it will feel like there is a switch that takes you between Authentic Self and personality, and it happens in a second. One moment you will be able to be authentic and the truth will be quite clear, and the next, your personality will take charge and you will want to react from an old, unhelpful pattern. The more you build the muscle for being authentic, the more easily you will sense when this switch is operating and will be able to bring yourself back, over and over again, to living as your Authentic Self.

FOSTERING PERSONAL CLARITY IN OTHERS

Motivation also refers to the ability of authentic leaders to foster balanced motivation in others.

Authentic Leaders take the time to know other people and are curious about what motivates them. They encourage employees, for example, to share their values and life visions in order to understand how best to support them to be successful. Authentic leaders look for opportunities to showcase others' performances, and their ability to self-manage allows them to let go of old unhelpful thoughts and behaviours that might otherwise get in the way of this (for example, the habit of taking the credit for others' work).

EMPATHY

Being authentic also supports having empathy—the ability, during interactions, to step into other people's shoes and consider their needs and expectations, and what they are thinking, feeling and sensing. This may be something that comes naturally, or a skill that requires constant revisiting and practice.

In a busy world full of multi-tasking, fast-paced days, and an increasing number of virtual interactions, being able to consider other people's personalities and emotions will support your effectiveness as a leader. Authentic leaders are able to override personal needs to consider others in their decisions.

Authentic Leaders learn to self-manage to let go of impatience and annoyance when a person comes to them with an urgent request. They are able to put down the smart phone, let go of what they are working on, and focus completely on the person before them. This is particularly helpful when giving feedback. If a leader lacks empathy they run the risk of shutting the other person down. But by considering the recipient's emotions, giving feedback can be a much more positive experience for all involved.

Alternatively, Authentic leaders honor their own needs when their old pattern might have been to help others at too high a cost to themselves. If they are working on a personal deadline and another approaches them for help, authentic leaders can set a boundary and ask a person to come back at a later time.

EXCEPTIONAL SOCIAL SKILLS

Business (and life) success is based on the ability to be in relationship with others. Authentic leaders have exceptional social skills for building long-term, trust-based relationships.

Authentic leaders enjoy relationships for what they are and are able to interact with others with mutual respect, integrity, and empathy. Authentic leaders understand the impacts they are having on others. They know how to create the conditions for others to feel comfortable around them, by being approachable, humble, and real in their interactions.

Authentic leaders enter into relationships for the long term; they establish and build a foundation of trust and mutual respect, and they skillfully navigate through difficult times. Authentic leaders also set boundaries based on their values and the values of the company, and when there is a misalignment, they may end relationships.

In general, authenticity supports you to slow down and be intentional about every interaction in every relationship you are building.

ARE THEY THE SAME?

This is a question I'd like to leave you with.

The distinction for me is intent. When emotional and social intelligence is applied for life-affirming choices, it becomes the same as authentic leadership – leadership using inner clarity and purpose to make choices in the moment to do the right thing.

The more you can self-regulate (self-manage) to override your ego/personality to do the right, ethical thing, in the moment, the more you cultivate peace for yourself, those you directly impact, and those who your positive ripple effect reaches globally. This is the goal of authentic leadership.

My question is – Is emotional and social intelligence focused always on the positive or is the awareness used to manipulate? It may be a rhetorical question and I'd still like to ask it.

Authentic leadership says choose life affirming decisions and activities; does emotional and social intelligence always point to this as well?

SUMMARY

By adopting the practices outlined within this book, authentic leaders will develop their emotional and social intelligence. Congruent with Daniel Goleman's model, authentic leaders are self-aware, able to self-regulate (or self-manage) and deeply intrinsically motivated. They are able to foster balanced motivation in others, to practice empathy, and, with exceptional social skills, to build long-lasting relationships. A question for you to ponder – Is authentic leadership and emotional and social intelligence the same thing? Authentic leadership says choose life affirming decisions and activities; does emotional and social intelligence always point to this as well?

CHAPTER EIGHT:
THE AUTHENTIC YOU™ PERSONAL PLANNING SYSTEM

What would it be like to have an inner guidance system,
available to you in each moment, in which the mechanism
that keeps you grounded and clear is your Authentic Self?

ORGANIZATIONAL PLANNING SYSTEMS

In organizations, strategic planning takes place on at least an annual basis. Executives gather to reflect on the context for the organization including the vision, values, strategies, measures and targets. This then cascades to individuals within the organization to set the focus for their activities for the year.

PERSONAL PLANNING SYSTEMS

In order to be an authentic leader, it is helpful to have a similar system—one that helps you remember who you are when at your best, with a clear personal vision for your life in mind. The Authentic You™ Personal Planning System is like strategic planning for the individual. This system has been used successfully for years, supporting countless numbers of people on their journey as authentic leaders.

The purpose of the system is for you, as a leader, to become clear about your inner guidance, and to create an awakening that will support you to take your Authentic Leadership to the next level. It begins with an orientation to who you are as your Authentic Self and continues from there.

Once you are clear about who you are when at your best, you will no longer be guided by the "shoulds" of personality (I should be doing *this* or people will think badly of me; I should be considering *that* or I won't make any money, etc.). As a result, you will bring a fresh, new perspective to the subsequent steps of the system.

The system can be used annually, or whenever it feels like time to step back and reflect. It is used to create an awakening as you discover or re-discover who you are at your best, and what is truly important to you at this stage in your life.

In this chapter we introduce the nine steps in the Authentic You™ Personal Planning System:

1. Remember your Authentic Self (page 82)
2. Articulate your values (page 91)
3. Discover your purpose (page 97)
4. Clarify your leadership principles (page 102)
5. Discover your life vision (page 106)
6. Assess your work-life balance (page 109)
7. Understand your awakening and the implications for your leadership (page 117)
8. Set your goals (page 119)
9. Create your inner development plan (page 122)

Each step is described in detail and includes examples and exercises for you to complete.

Note: Some of the information you develop will remain relatively stable over the years, providing inspirational guideposts (Authentic Self, values, purpose, and life vision). Other aspects may change frequently as you make course corrections for your day-to-day activities. These include your life vision (life vision is included in both categories as it may stay stable once you've found where you "fit" in the world, or it could change as you choose to create a different theme for your life), your work-life balance assessment, your goals, and your inner development plan.

PREPARING TO BEGIN

Before starting each step of the Authentic You™ Personal Planning System, it can be helpful to center yourself, allowing yourself to open to what will arise.

One of my favorite exercises is Kate Sutherland's "Groundwork"[46]. The following exercise was taken, with her permission, directly from her book *Make Light Work: 10 tools for inner knowing*[47]. This exercise also makes a wonderful a daily practice.

Groundwork, by Kate Sutherland

Centre through self-awareness - Being self-aware is synonymous with being centered, even if one is emotionally agitated. Being centered is a key part of the foundation for effective inner work.

Set Intention - Once I am centered I set an overarching intention: "May everything that comes through me serve the highest." You may say serve God or Gaia, or Truth or Love—whatever words work for you. Saying or thinking either phrase immediately shifts my center of gravity away from ego-driven, small "s" self to big "S" Self, a point of awareness that is interconnected with all that is.

Open - After setting intention, the next step is to become open or receptive. Inner work involves opening to our inner wisdom and truth, to another perspective. We only benefit from inner work tools if we are open to the gifts they bring us. Put another way, I do not engage in inner work unless I am committed to acting on what I get.[48]

Use this practice at the beginning of each of the steps to create the optimal conditions for your discoveries about yourself.

LEARNING TOOLS

Some steps in the system require writing and reflection, while others are about making changes in your life, both internally and externally. For the writing portion of the work, it is important to have the right tools—tools that reflect who you are and how you like to learn.

---

46   Kate Sutherland, *Make Light Work—10 Tools for Inner Knowing* (Vancouver: Incite Press, 2010) p 21 – 23.

47   For more on Kate's work or to purchase a copy of her book, see www. makelightwork.org.

48   Ibid, p 21—23.

Are you a visual learner or do you prefer the written word? Do you like to work on paper, or would you prefer to use your computer? The following is a list of tools you will need each time you complete the Authentic You™ Personal Planning System:

Tool:	When you use it:	Comments:
Action worksheets for each of the nine steps of the Authentic You™ Personal Planning System (See Appendix A)	Use these to work through the first draft of all of the exercises for each of the nine steps of the Authentic You™ Personal Planning System	Use each time you complete the steps for the Authentic You™ Personal Planning System, or for each participant when using this tool as a group.
Authentic You™ Personal Learning Journal (download for FREE)	Use this to record the final product of what you learn in each step	Download this FREE Companion Document from the www.leadauthentic.com. It is available for you to download and use each time you complete the steps of the Authentic You™ Personal Planning System
Authentic You™ Poster (Purchase a blank poster board paper in a colour that feels right for you, at an art supply or dollar store)	Use this as an alternative to record the final product of what you learn in each step.	Post on your wall so you can see all the information at a glance. Remember to leave enough space for each of the steps as you record your information.
Life-vision board (Purchase a blank poster board paper in a colour that feels right for you, at an art supply or dollar store)	Create this in Step Five of the Authentic You™ Personal Planning System	Two options for you: Option One—Create a paper version to post on your wall so you can see it at a glance. Option Two—Create an electronic version online using one of the tools or apps that is available, such as O Dream Board site (by Oprah Winfrey).

OTHER RESOURCES

There are many resources that will be helpful to you. A list of some of these is included for you in the bibliography at the end of this book.

SUMMARY

As organizations have strategic planning systems to set a course for moving forward and to provide focus for all employees, so too it is helpful for individual leaders to establish their inner guidance system for authenticity. The Authentic You™ Personal Planning System includes the following nine steps:

1. Remember your Authentic Self
2. Articulate your values
3. Discover your purpose
4. Clarify your leadership principles
5. Discover your life vision
6. Assess your work-life balance
7. Understand your awakening and the implications for your leadership
8. Set your goals
9. Create your inner development plan

There are additional tools you will use including action worksheets, the Authentic You™ Personal Learning Journal, and the Authentic You™ Poster and Life-vision board. You can choose the format—with paper and pen, or paperless—that feels right for you. In addition, a centering practice called "Groundwork" is provided to support you to relax and be open to new possibilities when completing each step.

STEP #1 -
REMEMBER YOUR AUTHENTIC SELF

"It can be more difficult to know ourselves than to know our friends"[49]

YOUR POTENTIAL

Take a deep breathe and imagine what it would be like to accept and embrace all of yourself—to have awareness of your gifts, to accept and to optimize who you are. What would it be like to be aware of it all and to live deliberately, in alignment with your Authentic Self: who you are when at your best? How would it be to say to yourself, "Ah, yes, this is who I am!", to feel comfortable in your skin, and to have clarity of your truth as you live and lead each day?

"When we are Present, there is something in us that feels compassionate and strong, patient and wise, indomitable and of great value. This something is who we actually are. It is the "I" beyond name, without personality—our True Nature." [50]

> **Authentic Self is your true nature. It is who you are when at your best—a creative and compassionate person with the unique qualities that make you who you are. Authentic Self is guided by intrinsic motivation, personal clarity and ethics. It is your potential and your birthright.**

We are not always aware of our own potential. Authentic leaders have the awareness to know they do not always see what is right in front of them. This is particularly the case when knowing their selves.

This is a reminder that you may need to travel in new territory to be open to listening to those around you to truly see who you are. Others act as mirrors for you. They see your potential—your light. Authentic leaders allow themselves to see—and even more to embrace, accept, and to settle into—the calmness, joy and inner clarity about who they are.

---

49   Source Unknown.

50   Riso and Hudson, *The Wisdom of the Enneagram,* p. 37.

Our deepest fear: Our deepest fear is not that we are inadequate. Our deepest fear is that we are powerful beyond measure. It is our light not our darkness that most frightens us. We ask ourselves, who am I to be brilliant, gorgeous, talented and fabulous? Actually, who are you not to be? You are a child of God. Your playing small doesn't serve the world. There's nothing enlightened about shrinking so that other people won't feel insecure around you. We were born to make manifest the glory of God that is within us. It's not just in some of us; it's in everyone. And as we let our own light shine, we unconsciously give other people permission to do the same. As we are liberated from our own fear; our presence automatically liberates others. – Marianne Williamson

"As you let your own light shine…" This light is your potential! In this book it's called Authentic Self—who you truly are without the limiting aspects of personality.

Authentic leaders understand their potential. They practice reconnecting with, and living more of the time as, their Authentic Self each day. In order for you to be able to do this, it can be helpful to first articulate the nature of your Authentic Self. Once articulated, you can spend time reflecting on it, to remember and begin to notice these attributes in your self. As you undertake a life-long practice and gain new awareness about your Authentic Self, you can learn to shift your perspective about different aspects of your personality, and take action, ever more authentically, on a day-to-day basis.

Think about how much time you spend criticizing yourself up about who you are and how much better you could be. There is an imbalance in self-judgment and skepticism, and even self-meanness (i.e. the inner critic), that makes it difficult to be objective and kind to your self.

Ongoing self-judgment can have an impact on your life and your leadership in ways that you may have no current awareness of. The goal of authenticity is to see the challenging aspects of your personality for what they are, to shift perspective, and to let them go in order to be more objective, and effective, in the moment.

AUTHENTIC SELF—WHY START HERE?

The way you treat others can be a reflection of how you treat yourself. It is therefore important to first know yourself and to treat yourself with respect and integrity, before you can have respect and integrity in your relationships.

When life is going well it can be simple and easy. When life gets challenging, however, is when it is especially helpful to have a tool kit for support. A personal planning system (the components of which we are covering in the balance of this chapter) provides this kit. It also requires a starting point—an anchor. We begin with your Authentic Self because it provides a point of reference that may be different from how you are used to seeing yourself on a day-to-day basis. It is your potential. When you see the best in yourself and remember what your potential is, you make different choices throughout the day.

Example: You may be frustrated and over-tired and find yourself being short in your tone and manner with employees. By just slowing down and remembering who you are when at your best, you can re-program your mind to make the choice to practice empathy, and to take the time to listen to their requests. This change in the moment, in your demeanor and behaviour, can be the difference between an employee feeling their work is important or their work doesn't matter, not to mention their personal feeling of whether or not they are important to you.

The same kinds of situations can arise with everyone you interact with: peers, customers, senior leaders or board members.

EXERCISES FOR ARTICULATING YOUR AUTHENTIC SELF

In order to articulate your Authentic Self you will start by doing research about who you are when at your best. This can be difficult for you to admit. And if you do, it may feel arrogant to put the words down on a piece of paper and accept them.

You will start by gathering information from several sources, including people who know you, personality assessments, as well as exercises and personal reflection. Your research may include the following four exercises:

- Review your life history to date (jobs, education, life steps)
- Complete a 360 Review
- Talk to your family and friends
- Use a personality or other self-assessment tool

CHAPTER EIGHT: THE AUTHENTIC YOU™ PERSONAL PLANNING SYSTEM

Use the action worksheet for articulating your Authentic Self (included in Appendix A) and the instructions below to complete the exercises that feel right for you. Once you have completed them, create a list of the words that describe your Authentic Self, and transfer the information to your Authentic You™ Personal Learning Journal and/or your Authentic You™ Poster.

1. Review your life to date

The first exercise is a personal reflection and review of your life.

Authentic leaders know their "story" and respect it and honor it for what it is—their interpretation of their lives to this point. They realize that much of their lives has been based on personality and lived on autopilot (i.e. they have been unaware or not conscious), and that this has only served them to a certain point.

Authentic leaders learn from the layers of their story each time a new one comes into their awareness. There are important lessons to be aware of, to understand, to accept and sometimes to heal, in order to move forward.

As you awaken to the unhelpful aspects of your personality, you are able to let go of old behaviours and thoughts when you need to, so you can focus on your strengths. A life review is a wonderful place to start. It is your story of where you came from (literally and metaphorically), what happened over the years, how you were successful, your relationships with others, and what you learned.

As you lay out your life, it helps to reflect on whether what you did was fulfilling or not. For each stage, ask yourself did it feed my soul? Did it "jazz" me? Did it raise my energy levels or diminish them?

It can also be helpful to understand your attitude at each stage in your life, and how you would describe yourself when you were feeling most fulfilled. These are some of the words that will be useful to describe your Authentic Self.

The following is an example of the first few steps in a life history review. A blank form is included in the Authentic Self action worksheet in Appendix A.

Your age or the year (approx.):	Life steps / Job or Position / Educational Training:	Level of fulfillment you experienced during this time. Show visually with one or more of each (+) or (-):	Words to describe your way of being when you were most fulfilled:
18	Finished high school	-	
25	Writer for local newspaper	+++	Courageous Curious Empathetic
33	Got divorced	---------	

2. Receive a 360-degree Review at Work

In organizations there is a process used for talent management, leadership development, performance management and succession planning called a 360-Degree Review. It is a process for asking for "real" feedback about strengths and opportunities for development in your leadership. It can be very helpful and is delivered either online or face-to-face. If online, raters complete a survey and a report is generated. If face-to-face, an Executive Coach or other Leadership Development expert interviews a number of people whom you work with, whom you work for, and who work for you, as well as your significant other, friends and family (where appropriate). The output is a 360-degree view of how others experience you. If you have not had one completed through work, you can complete one on your own by asking friends and family. This is described in the next exercise.

Participants may be asked about your strengths, opportunities for development and levels of emotional and social intelligence, all in the context of the organizational strategy, competencies and leadership development framework. The information is then compiled anonymously (if requested) and reflected back to you in a respectful and clear way.

If your organization supports your development, ask if they will arrange for you to receive a 360-Degree Review. You can then incorporate this into your Authentic You™ Personal Planning System. The personal planning system content can then inform your organizational requirements for Career Development including your Personal Performance Plan, as well.

It is invaluable to have the people who know you best provide insights to an objective interviewer in a way that is safe and supportive. While it is humbling and a bit daunting to hear real feedback about the good and the not so good, if you choose to see it as a learning experience it can be quite a gift! This gift often begins the process for personal and leadership transformation and the journey back to living as Authentic Self.

3. Conduct a 360 Review yourself

Another way to understand your potential is to talk to those people who are closest to you and who know you best, those people who care and will take the time to share their thoughts with you. Ask three or four people—your family, colleagues, friends, boss and team to write down the answers to the following questions:

Who am I when at my best? What are the words you would use to describe me when I am at my best?

What are my gifts in the world? How can you see me contributing? What, of the things that I can do and that I love, would help others most?

If you have a strong inner critic (and I have met very few people who don't) it can be difficult for you to take in this kind of feedback[51]. Take a deep breath and notice how it feels for you to simply accept the gift of it.

By having it written down, you can revisit your friends' and family's insights over the years in order to help you remember your potential. This is also a wonderful exercise to do for others at the same time. They answer the questions for you and you answer the questions for them, and then you read them aloud to each other.

The following table shows an example of responses from four people whom one participant asked: "Who am I when at my best?"

51   A side note regarding your inner critic and how it may show up when working with Personality-assessment tools. The inner critic may want to focus on the challenges, things that are wrong with the type you may be given. It will make judgments and can shut down your learning if you focus immediately on these aspects. While they are helpful to be aware of, it is important to focus first on your potential and Authentic Self in order to anchor your experience and Awareness here.

- Respondent one: Loving, Caring, Strategic, Driven, Visionary
- Respondent two: Loyal, Funny, Caring, Achiever
- Respondent three: Great father, Approachable, Get's results, Grounded, Humorous
- Respondent four: Hilarious, Inspiring, Visionary, Humble

Once you have written down the words that others have shared with you, take a few moments and reflect on what you are learning. Look for consistency and themes and check in with yourself about what feels true for you. It can be quite powerful to feel seen by others and to have them be a mirror for your Authentic Self.

4. Use a Personality or other Self-Assessment Tool

You may have been introduced to self-assessments at work or in leadership and/or personal development programs. Some examples include the Riso-Hudson Enneagram Type Indicator, Myers Briggs Type Indicator Assessment (MBTI)®, Insight Inventory®, Strengthsfinder Assessment, TTI Emotional Quotient Assessment, Authentic Leadership 360 Assessment, etc.

There are many other programs available and you can choose to use one (or more) if it feels right for you. Each program provides a different perspective on your self and your personality, highlighting which traits may be helpful, and which may be getting in your way.

USING THE ENNEAGRAM TO DISCOVER YOUR POTENTIAL

One personality assessment that fits particularly well with understanding your potential is the Enneagram Personality System. (It may resonate for you or it may not. The beauty is that there are others available if it doesn't. If it does, read on.)

While similar to other personal development systems and self-assessments such as Myers Briggs Type Indicator ® (MBTI) or Insights, the Enneagram differs in some important ways. Its purpose is to: "[invite] us to look deeply into the mystery of our true identity. It is meant to initiate a process of inquiry that can lead us to a more profound truth about ourselves and our place in the world."[52]

---

52   Riso and Hudson, *The Wisdom of the Enneagram*, p 7.

The Enneagram is a system for leadership and personal development that crosses genders and cultures, and focuses on the discovery of who we are when we are living to our potential.

"The modern Enneagram of personality type has been synthesized from many different spiritual and religious traditions. Much of it is a condensation of universal wisdom, the perennial philosophy accumulated by Christians, Buddhists, Muslims (especially the Sufis), and Jews (in the Kabbalah) for thousands of years."[53]

More recently it was paired with psychological theory in the early 1950's and later, by Oscar Ichazo and Claudio Naranjo as well as by Don Richard Riso and Russ Hudson, authors of *The Wisdom of the Enneagram*. They write, "The Enneagram can help us see what prevents us from remembering this deep truth about who we really are ….It does this by providing highly specific insights into our psychological and spiritual makeup."[54]

There are nine personality types in the system; each of us tends to associate with one type more strongly than the others. This system is used for individuals to discover their type, to understand their potential as a healthy functioning person, and then to develop competencies in areas where they might be underdeveloped. In this way they become more balanced and able to live aligned with their Authentic Self (or essence), more of the time.

Riso and Hudson's book on the Enneagram is a resource for a life-long practice of authenticity. Their description of the ten developmental levels for each of the types provides a map from the lowest, or unhealthy, behaviours to the most healthy. The highest level of development provides a unique picture of a person's potential—specific to their personality type as described by the Enneagram. They also provide descriptions of what it is like to transform to the highest level of potential, and the exercises that can be helpful.

SUMMING IT UP: NOW DESCRIBE YOUR AUTHENTIC SELF

Reflect on all of the information you have gathered, including your own thoughts and reflections, and compile a list of words that describe you at your best. Three examples of wording for three different people's Authentic Self are shown below. Notice the distinction between the three and how you get a sense of the person from each list:

---

53   Ibid, p 9.

54   Ibid, p 24.

- Authentic Self descriptive words for Person one: Courageous, Loyal, Strategic, Warm, Approachable, Funny, Helpful
- Authentic Self descriptive words for Person two: Calm, Poised, Self-confident, Driven, Visionary, Grateful, Entrepreneur
- Authentic Self descriptive words for Person three: Direct, Loyal, Gets things done, Intensely committed, Witty, Inventor

NEXT STEPS:

Transfer your description of your Authentic Self to your Authentic You™ Personal Learning Journal and/or Authentic You™ Poster. Bring your Authentic Self description and mindset into each of the following steps in the Authentic You™ Personal Planning System. It will add fresh insight and perspective as you consider and complete each one.

STEP #2 - ARTICULATE YOUR VALUES

Authentic leaders have a clear "internal North Star or moral compass"[55] that guides their choices each day. These leaders listen closely to the messages that come from within.

UNDERSTANDING VALUES

Values—what are they? A few words on an organization's website that the C-Suite (executives) put together for window dressing and then never revisit? Or are they guideposts that provide support for decision making and leading that are referred to regularly and integrated into all parts of the business? As a leader, have you ever articulated your own values? Do you know what they are? These are distinct from the values of your organization (which guide the behaviours for employees).

Your values are deeply held beliefs about what is important to you for your life—all parts of it.

They include words that describe what is most important to you. They are your bottom line. Values are "believed to be what people care about deeply and serve as standards for judging acts, guiding behavior, evaluating social conditions, and give meaning to life. Values are thought to be relatively stable, much longer lasting and less subject to change than opinions so that they are not subject to sudden shifts or impulses of the moment."[56]

Values can also be prioritized to give emphasis to different ones at different times in your life.

Living congruent with your values means that in each moment and with each decision you are leading and creating your life in alignment with who you truly are. If you are living aligned with your values, you will feel

---

55   Bill George, True North – *Discover your Authentic Leadership* (San Francisco: Josey Bass, 2007), p xxiii.

56   Source: Values, http://www.orednet.org/~jflory/205/205_val_intro.htm

different than if you are not. When aligned, you may experience a sense of inner peace, happiness and fulfillment. When you are living out of alignment you may notice a different feeling—frustration, overwhelm, burnout, a grey cloud of depression or a knot in your stomach.

VALUES AND PERSONAL GUIDANCE

Your values can support you in making decisions on a day-to-day basis—particularly when you are not sure how to proceed. In today's fast-paced world, where ambiguity abounds, values can be essential! There will be times when you'll encounter difficult situations that require choice and action that isn't always easy. And there will be times when opportunity requires choice as well. Some of these situations at work include:

- You may be developing a new product and service in a completely new situation in which the parameters and use for the product or service are completely new.
- You may see a co-worker behave in a way that is unethical.
- You may be faced with an incredible opportunity and need to make a decision that could change your life.
- You may be approached by a supervisor in a way that you are not comfortable with.
- You may be put in a situation that could create a conflict of interest.
- When under stress or having a bad day, you may behave in a way that isn't congruent with your values. You may make a mistake and not even realize it after you've done it.
- You may be feeling out of balance and overwhelmed and need a way to check in with yourself.

Your values will help you understand and navigate the trade offs[57] in your day-to-day situations.

---

57   There may be situations where you are unsure how to proceed, even when you are clear that they are outside of your values and you are uncomfortable with them. If you work for a company with a Respectful Workplace or Code of Conduct Advisor, call them. Ask your boss or HR rep for confidential advice. If you work in an organization where you do not have these resources, call a friend who is (or who knows) a lawyer or someone who has role-modeled high ethical standards and ask them for support. Call the labour relations board or other advisory body. They can provide thoughtful insights and an objective perspective for what could be a stressful, complex situation. And you can take the guidance that feels right and still make the final decision yourself—again checking in with your values for how to proceed with the final steps.

Example: You are presented with a new business or job opportunity and are unsure if it is right for you. You can use your values as criteria to evaluate the opportunity. If it is a position requiring 80 hours a week including travel around the world and your values include travel and adventure, then it might be the right position for you. If you value spending time with your family as you have young children, then it might not be. Or it might be a great opportunity that fits your values, just not the right time.

EXERCISES FOR CLARIFYING YOUR PERSONAL VALUES

This section contains the following three exercises for articulating your personal values:

1. Reflect on past situations when you had to step back and make important trade-offs and when you had to dig deep into your beliefs to make the final decisions.
2. Review a list of values words—and select the ones that resonate for you.
3. Test out the values—reflect on possible situations in the future and how you will make your decisions, both at work and in your personal life.

The exercises are described in detail below. Use the action worksheet included in Appendix A to record your research and articulate your values.

1. Reflect on past situations and trade offs

There have been times in your leadership career and your life when you may have needed to stop and consider what steps to take next. These could range from making a decision about a new career opportunity to whether to go to university, or when to have a family. Each day, we encounter situations that require us to make decisions, and our values—whether we know them overtly, or consider them intuitively—are providing the guideposts.

Think of a situation in which you have had to take time to reflect on a decision, basing it on your deeply held convictions about what the right answer would be. A decision, for example, in which you needed to decide whether to take a promotion which would require much more time at work and travel that would take you away from your family for the equivalent of 5 months a year.

93

Write down words that describe what you believe in that has lead you to make these decisions. For example: importance of family; love of travel; love of work; stimulation of adventure.

2. Review a list of values words:

After reflecting on what values are, and some situations in your life that have required trade-offs based on what is deeply important to you, it is time to choose the words that describe your values. Having a list of words for your values can be helpful, particularly if you are a visual learner or if you have not considered values before.

The following is a list of common personal values:[58]

Accomplishment, Success	Flair	Progress
Accountability	Freedom	Prosperity, Wealth
Accuracy	Friendship	Punctuality
Adventure	Fun	Quality of work
All for one & one for all	Global view	Regularity Resourcefulness
Beauty	Good will	Respect for others
Calm, quietude, peace	Goodness	Responsiveness
Challenge	Gratitude	Results-oriented
Change	Hard work	Rule of Law
Cleanliness, orderliness	Harmony	Safety
Collaboration	Honesty	Satisfying others
Commitment	Honor	Security
Communication	Independence	Self-givingness
Community	Inner peace, calm, quietude	Self-reliance
Competence	Innovation	Service
Competition	Integrity	(to others, society)
Concern for others	Justice	Simplicity
Content over form	Knowledge	Skill
Continuous improvement	Leadership	Speed

---

58   Source: Values, http://www.gurusoftware.com/GuruNet/Personal/Topics/Values.htm
For a list of Business values see: http://www.gurusoftware.com/GuruNet/Business/Values.htm

Cooperation	Love, Romance	Spirit in life (using)
Coordination	Loyalty	Stability
Country, love of (patriotism)	Maximum utilization	Standardization
Creativity	(of time, resources)	Status
Customer satisfaction	Meaning	Strength
Decisiveness	Merit	Succeed; A will to-
Delight of being, joy	Money	Success, Achievement
Democracy	Openness	Systemization
Discipline	Peace, Non-violence	Teamwork
Discovery	Perfection (e.g. of details)	Timeliness
Ease of Use	Personal Growth	Tolerance
Efficiency	Pleasure	Tradition
Equality	Positive attitude	Tranquility
Excellence	Power	Trust
Fairness	Practicality	Truth
Faith	Preservation	Unity
Family	Privacy	Variety
Family feeling	Problem Solving	Wisdom

The following are examples of values for three different people:
- Person A: Adventure, travel, volunteering, relationships, financial freedom, fun
- Person B: Wellness, integrity/authenticity, family/relationships, ease/savoring/joy, being in-service to others
- Person C: Financial security, spirituality, education, family, environmental stewardship

For another great exercise to clarify and rank your values, see the following values Worksheet at http://mikedesjardins.com/tag/core-values/.

3. Test out your values

Once you have written down your values, it can be helpful to test them out to see if you have missed anything and to see how they provide guidance in different situations.

Think of several situations at work and in your personal life in which you need to make an important decision.

Example One: You are returning to work after maternity leave and you want to be effective as a leader, as well as with your family, and maintain your wellness.

Example Two: you need to decide on a new product offering at work that may have potential negative impacts on a business partner.

For each of your own situations, reflect on your values and what guidance they provide you. List them in order of importance to get even clearer about the emphasis you want to place on different parts of your life. Make any adjustments to your values based on what you have learned.

The following shows an example of a person's values as well as a situation in which they are using those values to make decisions:

- Values (in order of importance: family, wellness, career, education, spirituality, fun
- Situation: (Mary is returning to work after maternity leave) Mary's value of family (first priority) means that she may only want to work four days a week; her value for wellness means that she will make time for rest by booking time at the gym 3x/week for "me" time; and her value of education will have to drop in priority as she forgoes the MBA she has been thinking of doing, for the foreseeable future.

Remember, this first articulation of your values is just a starting point and your values may evolve. They may also change in order of importance at different times in your life. For example, one person values travel and working hard. After they have children, they have a new value of time with family. Their focus has changed and family time "trumps" travel for the first few years of raising their children. Alternatively, they may incorporate travel into their lives in a new way—instead of travelling internationally, they may choose to travel close to home, or in a way that the children can participate.

NEXT STEPS:

After you have articulated and tested your values, transfer them to your Authentic You™ Personal Learning Journal and/or Authentic You™ Poster. Bring them, as well as the words describing you as your Authentic Self, and move on to the next step: discover your purpose.

STEP #3 –
DISCOVER YOUR PURPOSE

WHAT ARE YOU HERE TO DO?

What were you intended for on this earth? What is your gift to share with others? What is your purpose?

Authentic leaders are clear about what their higher purpose is, what they were intended for in their leadership and their life. Your purpose may be broader than the current role you are in and will be applicable across time, audiences and industries. If your current role is aligned with your Authentic Self, it will fit within your purpose.

Your purpose is the reason beyond yourself that provides meaning for your life. It is how you are meant to leave your mark in the world—how you are meant to contribute, and your legacy.

By being clear on your purpose, you can stay focused—with determination and discipline—even on the days when you are frustrated or overwhelmed and would like to be doing anything else but what you are doing. You will experience a new sense of effectiveness and inner peace when you live each day aligned to your Authentic Self. You will be contributing in a way that is beneficial for all: it feeds your soul and is also of value for your customers, team, organization, community, and the world.

Clarity about your purpose may take time, and can be an iterative process. Some people are clear from a very young age. For example Sophia, aged 10, knows she wants to be a doctor and save lives; Paul knows he wants to help make people happy by creating video games. Others may need to have several chapters in their lives before they come to the point of understanding what they are meant to do.

For example, an executive who is a CFO, after losing a good friend to cancer, decides to leave the corporate world to dedicate her/his life to building homes in developing countries. A teacher and at some point gets bored with his/her career and it loses its meaning. She/he then becomes a consultant on a part-time basis and at the same time spends years compiling a genealogy book for his/her children to know more about their lineage.

While you are exploring your purpose, notice how your inner critic may appear and say things like "this is a stupid exercise—you'll never be able to make money at that". For now, see if you can suspend these judgments. At this stage you are just getting an idea of the things you love to do.

Often I hear people say, "I don't know what my gift is". Further into the conversation their faces light up when they remember an aspect of their life, often something they are doing as a hobby that they are passionate about. Some examples include:

- "I love making jewelry."
- "I like to help others achieve their dreams."
- "I like to share joyful memories with others—usually involving outdoor adventure."
- "People over the years have said I'm good at giving detailed feedback that helps people take their performance to the next level."
- "I'm really good at negotiating and relationship building."

DREAM BIG

What would it be like to do what you love and to believe that abundance will follow?[59]

Authentic leaders have done their personal work to the point where the major limiting beliefs they have experienced in life are now in the past. The old beliefs are no longer clouding their knowledge of what they love to do. Understanding your purpose also means researching how you can make money while you are also being helpful in the world. This is the sweet-spot of living authentically. It involves being clear and choiceful about how you contribute, ensuring that it is aligned with who you truly are and what feeds your soul, as well as what will bring you abundance (in whatever form is meaningful for you).

Dreaming big means that you take off the blinders and let go of any resistance you may have. You allow yourself to see possibilities for yourself that others around you can probably already see. By doing some simple research, paying attention to how you feel (where your energy builds and which activities you feel joyful when doing), and talking to those closest to you, you will discover the purpose for your life.

---

59 Many books have been written on this subject such as "Do what you love, the money will follow—Discovering Your Right Livelihood" by Marsha Sinetar.

EXERCISES TO CLARIFY YOUR PURPOSE

As a reminder, clarity about your purpose may take time and be an itera-tive process. Or you may already be in a role or living your life in a way that is aligned with your purpose. The following exercises will either validate it, or provide new possibilities for the next steps on your journey. Use the action worksheet that is included in Appendix A for completing the research and exercises for articulating your purpose.

In order to become clear about your purpose, there are several things you can do:

1. Spend time in self-reflection about what your purpose is
2. Conduct interviews with others who do what you think you might like to do
3. Shift or let go of self-limiting beliefs in order to see different possibilities

1. Spend time in self-reflection

Review your research from the first two steps: Remembering your Authen-tic Self—the life review; the information from friends, family, and co-workers; the results of your personality assessments; and articulating your values.

Reflect on how it feels to understand who you are at your best and what is important to you. Then, complete the following statements:

- My strengths are (what I'm good at and what I love)....
- When I do the following activities, I notice that my energy builds....
- I love contributing by doing the following....
- My passion in life is....

Record what you are learning as you complete each of these.

2. Conduct interviews

Conduct informal interviews with at least three people who are either leaders you admire or are living their lives and contributing in ways that you are curious about or interested in. By understanding the journeys of others, and what it is they are doing, you can more clearly understand what you are meant to do.

For example you know a person who has started a business in eco-tourism, a field you have always been curious about; this person's work is especially of interest as she is a former doctor, and she made her major life change in her late forties. Another person is a lawyer and you think you might like to be a lawyer and represent people when they have been in an accident. Another person has written a book about time management and effective organizing. Another makes jewellery for a living.

Whichever people you pick, ask them to have or tea or coffee with you. Ask if they will be willing to share their story and insights with you. Consider asking them one or all of the following questions and record your responses on the action worksheet for your purpose.

- Can you describe what it is that you do?
- How is what you do meaningful to you?
- How did you get to where you are? What has been your journey?
- What made you make the changes to your life?
- What are the things that I need to consider if I was to do something similar?
- What are the challenges with what you do?
- What do you love about living this way?
- What does a typical day in your life look like?
- What does the typical month look like?

After you have conducted the interviews, ask yourself the following questions:

- Does thinking about this as a possibility excite me for my life?
- Is there other information I need to gather about their occupation?
- Does my energy build or diminish when I hear about the way this person is living?

UNDERSTAND YOUR PURPOSE

Remind your inner critic that this is just a draft, so you can let go of the pressure for perfection. Combine what you have learned in the exercises described so far and jot them down as bullet points or statements.

Next combine these points into one statement. The following are examples of purpose for three different people:

- Person A: To support others to live their perfect blend of joy and success.
- Person B: To help save the environment through my actions and my work.
- Person C: To leave a legacy for my children.

3. Shift or Let go of Self-limiting Beliefs

You may have a difficult time seeing new possibilities for your leadership and your life if you can only imagine one way forward—the way it has always been—or if you notice that you have lots of reasons why something different is just not possible. If this is where you find yourself, you are not alone. Many people arrive at this place in their lives at some point. What may be helpful is to get support—either of a coach, counselor or thera-pist—in order to shift or let go of some of these current beliefs.

Example: You want to be a better leader and yet you find yourself constantly micromanaging your team members and overwhelmed from too much work. It might be helpful to learn to let go of any issues with control you might have, as well as to learn how you relate to trust and whether there are any opportunities for you to trust the people who work for you in a different way than you are currently doing.

If you sense you need to do some inner work before considering outer potentials, review the chapter on the inner development, as well as the ac-tion worksheet for creating your inner development plan (Appendix A). You may need to spend several months working on shifting beliefs before you can see different possibilities for your purpose. If you are not sure how to proceed, your inner development plan may include just one item—find a trusted person to give you support for a targeted period of time.

Once you have completed, say, three to six months of support, return to these exercises with a renewed openness to different possibilities that may come into your awareness.

NEXT STEPS

Once you have completed your purpose, leave it for a few days and adjust it until it feels aligned with who you are. When it represents your Authentic Self, you will experience a sense of calm and deep inner know-ing. It has been described as feeling like you have come home.

Transfer your purpose to your Authentic You™ Personal Learning Journal or Authentic You™ Poster, and go on to the next step—clarifying your leadership principles.

Note: If you are unsure about your purpose after reviewing this chap-ter, and you are going to work on shifting self-limiting beliefs, go on to Step #5 – Create your life-vision board. This exercise provides another way to begin to discover your purpose. In addition, you may want to set a goal or intention to research what others who have already found their purpose are doing. You would include this in Step #9 as you create your inner development plan.

STEP #4
CLARIFY YOUR LEADERSHIP PRINCIPLES

WHAT ARE LEADERSHIP PRINCIPLES?

Authentic leaders use leadership principles to live in alignment with their Authentic Self, their values, and their purpose on a day-to-day basis. Leadership principles have been described as "values translated into action".[60]

Leadership principles are statements that help to articulate how to translate Authentic Self, values, and purpose into your day-to-day activities.

Leadership principles are broad enough to cross industries and businesses, and specific enough to provide guidance for your day-to-day activities. They support you to tactically translate your personal clarity and intrinsic motivators, to being able to lead and live authentically. The following are examples of leadership principles for two different people:

Person One:

Authentic Self/ Purpose:	Value:	Leadership Principle:
Authentic Self: Creative, Entrepreneurial, Self-aware, Inspiring, Courageous **Purpose:** Supporting people to be the best they can be	Authenticity	Talk about the importance of authenticity when having conversations and model it in your leadership—both 1:1 and in groups; with peers, direct reports and supervisors; and with customers.

---

60   Bill George, True North, p 86.

	Sustainability	Creating the conditions for a low-to-no carbon footprint; modeling it in your own behaviours for your team and in your personal life.
	Connection	Facilitating team-building workshops where people can develop community as they learn about their potential as a person.

Person Two:

Authentic Self/Purpose:	Value:	Leadership Principle:
Authentic Self: Direct, Loyal, Gets things done, Intensely committed, Witty, Inventor **Purpose:** To leave a legacy for my children.	Financial security	Ensure the return on investment is clearly articulated and understood before the investment is agreed to. And Support team members to understand financial concepts and how they support decision making.
	Education	Creating the conditions for a life-long learning.
	Family	Encourage "family first" philosophy with my employees and clients.

Your Authentic Self description, values, purpose and leadership principles may hold relatively constant in your life. What may change over time are the specific jobs you choose in your career.

When you are clear about what is important to you, your criteria for choosing positions become clear as well. When in jobs that are congruent with your Authentic Self, you are more engaged and effective at what you do.

EXERCISE TO CLARIFY YOUR LEADERSHIP PRINCIPLES

There are several things you can do to clarify your leadership principles.

First, reflect on your what you've learned about your Authentic Self, values and purpose. Pay particular attention to the following questions:

- When I am being my Authentic Self, without the limiting voices of my personality, the "shoulds", or my inner critic, what is it that I love to do at work or in my business?
- What do I love to do that will support creating a great environment where people I work with can feel comfortable to be authentic as well?
- How will I contribute to making the world a better place through my business practices?
- How will these business practices contribute to abundance for the business, the world, and myself?

Once you have reflected on these questions, create a list of words or statements that are your leadership principles.

Using the list of leadership principles you created; plan to incorporate them into your day-to-day activities by listing your current job account-abilities and activities, and answering the following questions.

- What percentage of the activities I do each day are aligned with my principles?
- What can I do differently to bring a higher percentage of my day-to-day leadership activities into alignment with my leadership principles?
- Are there activities that do not align, that I can given away to someone else who likes to do them? Who else could do the activities for me?
- Is there any support I would need to have in order to implement my leadership principles?

Suggestions for incorporating your principles into your day-to-day leadership include:

- Review them with 1 or 2 trusted friends, family or peers and ask for feedback. Add anything you may have missed.

- Communicate these to your peers, boss and team.
- Integrate these principles and what you are learning about yourself into your organizational leadership development processes (talent management, performance management) annually.
- Use your Authentic Self description, values, purpose and principles to guide your career advancement.
- Practice leading using your principles.
- Adjust them as you evolve and grow.

NEXT STEPS

Once you have completed your leadership principles, leave them for a few days and make edits until they feel aligned with who you are.

When they are aligned with your Authentic Self, you will experience a sense of calm and deep inner knowing that you are on the right path.

Transfer your principles to your Authentic You™ Personal Learning Journal or Authentic You™ Poster, and go on to the next step—creating your life-vision board.

STEP #5
CREATE YOUR LIFE VISION

Authentic leaders have clarity of purpose and a personal vision for the way they live and lead. As they move through each day, they keep an eye on their life vision as an inspirational point on the horizon. This provides a creative tension that helps to focus day-to-day choice and action.

Your life vision is the articulation of what your optimal life looks like—both personally and at work.

What is your personal vision for your life? How do you want to live? What would it be like to be intentional about how you live and lead? Knowing the answers to these questions is the difference between living a life that happens to you and creating the life that you want to live.

Paint Cans

Paint cans, dip in, play with the colors of your life.

Paint a picture, paint a masterpiece.

Your life is your own creation, your own masterpiece.

Choose the colors with your heart. Discern what is true to you.

When you paint your life from your heart the most spectacular painting will appear.

Hang your painting up.

Some may say, "THIS IS MY PAINTING, THIS IS MY LIFE."

They believe this is the only painting they have. They build a house around this painting.

They might look at other people's paintings and say, "WOW, LOOK AT THEIR PAINTING. I LIKE THEIR PAINTING BETTER THAN MINE."

They don't like their own painting anymore. They become sad.

They need to remember that they still have all those paint cans in the closet. Millions of beautiful colors.

Paint a new masterpiece.

Paint over the old one if you like.

Better yet, paint many masterpieces and build your house out of the paintings instead of around just one.

Be free to create and create.

The color is your Essence and colors used to reflect you, should change and grow as you do.

You are the master of your creation. You are the master of creating your own masterpiece.

HAPPY PAINTING

Source: Claire McInnis

Your life vision can be created visually as a collage and/or by writing down the themes that emerge. You can complete it using a poster board and magazines or you can use online tools, such as the O Dream Board[61], as well. You could also write a poem or create a song. In short, use whatever creative modality will support you to express your optimal life! This is an important step to creating the life you choose to live.

After your life-vision board is created, you need only to spend time reflecting on it. This will guide you to choose and take steps that move your day-to-day experience into further alignment with your vision as your Authentic Self.

EXERCISE TO CREATE YOUR LIFE VISION BOARD

Use the following exercise, as well as the action worksheet in Appendix A to create your life-vision board. Here's how:

1. Gather 5 to 6 magazines that represent who you are at this point in your life, family photos that are meaningful (and can be cut up and/ or taped), and other materials that you might want to incorporate into a collage. Purchase a poster board (in a colour that speaks to you) and gather together a pair of scissors, some scotch tape, and some coloured pens.

   Put on your most comfortable clothing, find a space that feels energizing for you to create in, and put on your favourite music. Give yourself up to 2 hours (or whatever is needed) to create your life-vision board. Note: While this is a lovely exercise to do with your partner or significant other, it can be helpful to leave that for later. For now, the focus is creating your own life vision.

---

61   O Dream Boards, http://www.oprah.com/packages/o-dream-board.html

2. Flip through the magazines and other materials you have gathered, paying attention to images and words that call to you. This is a right-brain exercise so remind yourself to let go of analyzing for the moment as you enjoy creating. Cut the images and words out and set aside.

3. Once you have gathered all the images and words that feel right at this time, begin to assemble them on the poster board and tape them in place as a collage. After you are done, write your name and the date in one corner of the board so you remember when you created it. As you make more life-vision boards, you will be able to follow how they change over time.

4. Record the themes that emerged from this exercise in your Authentic You™ Personal Learning Journal.

Once you have completed your life-vision board, review it in its entirety and notice how you feel. Pay attention to any emotions that arise as you spend time with it for the first time. What are you learning about yourself as a result?

If and when you are comfortable, share it with someone you trust and admire and whom you want to involve as a support for your creation. Again, notice how it feels to practice being vulnerable and sharing something deeply important to you with another person.

Review your life-vision board on a regular basis (spend some time with it each week) and then put it away. This will help to anchor it into your awareness so you can let it "percolate" and provide guidance in the background.

When you have achieved a major milestone in your life (this may be years later), review the board again and see how your actions relate to the vision you created. It is common for people to share that they are amazed that something that they put on their life-vision board, and then completely forgot about, has come to fruition in their life at this time.

NEXT STEPS

Once you have completed your vision for your life, post it in a place where you can revisit it and spend time with it to keep it top of mind.

Now you are ready to use all the information you have developed as context to move to the next step and assess your current vs. optimal work-life balance.

STEP #6
ASSESS YOUR WORK-LIFE BALANCE

Authentic leaders are intentional about their work-life balance.

Work-life balance occurs when you have an understanding of the different parts of your life and the relative emphasis and time you would like to dedicate to each. This will be different over time as priorities and life changes.

Authentic leaders have a sense of calm about them. They are able to maintain perspective and balance all parts of their lives, more of the time. They have wellness practices that are foundational to their ability to maintain perspective, particularly in uncomfortable or new situations. Authentic leaders live and lead thoughtfully and make time for reflection and "white space" in their week. Their priorities for work-life balance change as they move through new chapters in their lives. Their sense of balance is flexible, knowing that in order to be in balance, they may first be out of balance—a reminder that progress is not just linear.

Mastering work-life balance can support authenticity. First take stock of your current life balance—how you think about it, and how you are balancing your time.

There are two things for you to consider:
1. What work-life balance is
2. The benefits of a healthy work-life balance.

1. WHAT IS WORK-LIFE BALANCE?

Work-life balance is three things:
1. A choice that you make in how you see the world
2. A "muscle" that you strengthen over time
3. A lifelong practice

Close your eyes and imagine a satellite picture of a hurricane. There is a whirling storm and circular cloud structure located around a central eye. Day-to-day life in the corporate world can be like this as well—the storms at work whirl frantically yet inside it there is an eye. In the eye it is calm.

It doesn't mean that the storm has stopped or slowed in intensity—on the contrary, the storm may continue for some time.

Authentic leaders learn to live life from the calmness of the eye and to dip in to the "busy-ness" of life when they need to. Around them, leaders who are less aware may be running (literally at times) from meeting to meeting, with the idea that, as leaders, they are indispensable. They may believe that if they aren't involved in everything, if they aren't at every meeting, the work won't get done effectively. Such leaders are often late for everything and never seem to have enough time. They choose to live in the frantic whirl of the storm.

Yet in each moment we get to choose—storm or eye.

There is a great booked called Slowing Down to the Speed of Life where the authors describe two modes of thinking—the processing, analytical, or task mode; and the free-flow, described as creative intelligence or effortless thinking.[62] They talk about the importance of learning to find a balance and to live using both—creative free-flow and analytical or task—in order to be more effective.

Western culture values and rewards the "getting things done" mode of tasks and so we learn to spend a large part of our lives in the analytical way of thinking. Yet when we re-learn how to spend time in the free-flow mode, we can tap more fully into creativity, wisdom and original thinking.

Example: Gerry is a senior business leader. Up until two years ago, he had no idea that he was living life frantically. He reflects for a moment and remembers that at its worst, he was sleeping five hours a night and sending emails to the team at four o'clock in the morning. That was a good day. On a bad day, he remembers getting up at twelve-thirty... a.m.

Gerry realizes that he had no idea how out of control he was until a friend at work sat him down and said, "You look like you have a huge weight on your shoulders—you know you don't have to do it all, you can ask for help." Gerry remembers not wanting to hear the message, thinking his friend was crazy and actually being angry at her. How dare she? He thought. Now when he looks back at it, he is so thankful for the wake-up call.

---

62   Richard Carlson, and Joseph Bailey, *Slowing down to the Speed of Life—How to create a more peaceful, simpler life from the inside out* (New York: HarperCollins Books, 1997), pp. 11 - 30.

*Gerry thought that if he wasn't "doing"—he called it "crank-
ing"—he was being unproductive and felt guilty.*

*After the wake-up call, his journey to living life with balance
began in earnest. The stakes got high enough on a personal level
when he began experiencing heart palpitations and constant
anxiety. He knew it was time to shift how he thought about, and
practiced, work-life balance.*

*It took Gerry more than 3 years to feel like he had a more bal-
anced life. His foundational practices, including meditation, have
been a savior for him. A simple daily sitting practice during the
week has helped him see his racing mind, develop the ability—in
a new or stressful situation—to stop, breathe, and clear his mind;
to get perspective and collect his thoughts.*

*Gerry has evolved many foundational practices for wellness:
running, yoga, hiking in nature, journaling and annual 10-day
meditation retreats. In the past, these were the first things to go
when he got busy and had to "get things done"—which was more
often the case than not.*

*What is different now is that he can see when he loses his balance
much more quickly than in the past. He is able to keep his foundational practices in place with more discipline when his life gets
busy, and when he gets completely overwhelmed, he asks for help
in order to make space for his wellness.*

Learning to live life from the place of the eye of the storm can be challenging as well as uncomfortable at times. You may have to re-learn how
to slow down your physical body and central nervous system, as you learn
about what the free-flow mode of thinking is.

Work-life balance is a "muscle" that we learn to strengthen over time. I
have worked with a great leader, a CEO of a multi-billion dollar firm, who
has demonstrated to me that balance is possible even when there are so
many possibilities for how to spend our time. Family, friends, careers, parents, projects, boards, work, exercise and training.... We each have many,
many things that we can choose to fill our time with.

You can sense a balanced leader as soon as you meet them—they are calm and relaxed. While they may be busy, they are not anxious or overwhelmed (at least not most of the time). One key difference between those who have balance and those who don't, is that those who have balance have figured out what it takes to live life from a place where they can see the frantic and either choose not to be in it, or choose when to be in it and when to pull out. They are able to care for themselves, manage stress effectively, and be consistent in their foundation as a person. When they get out of balance these leaders have learned to notice, to navigate trade-offs, and to return to a sense of balance more quickly than those who have not.

2. THE BENEFITS OF HEALTHY WORK-LIFE BALANCE

Work-life balance is an important practice for managing stress. Long-term stress has many implications—here are a few signs of stress in thinking, behavior, or mood. You may:

- Become irritable and intolerant of even minor disturbances.
- Feel irritated or frustrated, lose your temper more often, and yell at others for no reason.
- Feel jumpy or exhausted all the time.
- Find it hard to concentrate or focus on tasks.
- Worry too much about insignificant things.
- Doubt your ability to do things.
- Imagine negative, worrisome, or terrifying scenes.
- Feel you are missing opportunities because you cannot act quickly.[63]

Long-term stress also has implications for the immune system, cardiovascular disease and other health-related issues.[64]

On an airplane the flight attendant reviews what to do if the oxygen is cut off and tells you to first help yourself and then to help others. It is like this with your work-life balance. You have to first see the value of caring for yourself (and in some cases learn how to do it), so you have the capacity and resiliency to be of service to clients, peers and others.

Balance is a life-long practice—some weeks you may be happier with your progress than others. Relax into it—you're in it for the long term.

---

63   Effects of Stress, http://www.webmd.com/balance/stress-management/stress-management-effects-of-stress

64   Ibid.

Also, the context of your life changes with your priorities so work-life balance will need to be flexible and adjustable. Once you see a new possibility for how to think about balance, clarify what your values are and what is important to you, you can develop new awareness about yourself and the beliefs that might be limiting you, you can make different choices about what you let into your life and what you let go of. You can "practice" new habits to support it, more of the time.

Work-life balance has several benefits. It supports you to be a more effective leader, as you are able to live with integrity and be authentic in all parts of your life. It helps you to relax and minimize the distractions of stress, which is key to tapping into your free-flow mode of thinking, or your intuition. It supports you in being more productive as you have a clear mind more of the time—particularly when you need to navigate through new territory where creativity and original thought is needed—as well as to have more choice in how you respond to situations as they arise.

Work-life balance can mean improved quality of productivity and relationships as you are able to keep perspective in times of turmoil. Have you ever noticed the inefficiencies—some call it "spin"—that occur with team members who are under continuous stress? Work-life balance supports a focus on immediate priorities. As you start to manage situations in other parts of your life in a way that is true to who you are, you can minimize the time that you would normally spend distracted.

And finally, the practice of constantly navigating the trade-offs between personal life and work (as well as developing new, mutually beneficial solutions) can be seen as a microcosm for developing the competency for creating the new paradigms, in business and in organizations, that leaders are being called on to develop today.

Developing new paradigms requires creativity and original thought; creativity requires relaxation into free-flow thinking; and work-life balance is foundational to both.

EXERCISE TO ASSESS YOUR WORK-LIFE BALANCE

Complete your work-life balance Assessment using the sample shown below and the action worksheet included in Appendix A.

Example: Joan's work-life balance Assessment. This diagram shows the different aspects of Joan's life and the amount of effort and energy she is spending in each. The outside of the circle is the optimal level, while the point on each line for the pieces of the "pie" show the current levels for each area:

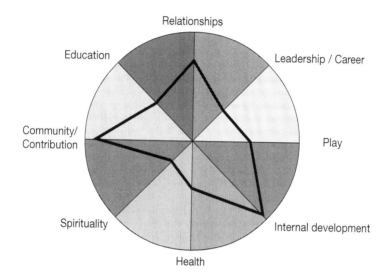

The assessment indicates the areas of her life where Joan may be feeling out of balance, and that she may want to make adjustments. It is evident that Joan is happy with the level of energy and time she spends on community and contribution, relationships and internal development, while she would like to focus more on health and spirituality.

This is a great exercise to return to whenever you are noticing that your balance is off. Each time that occurs—and it will, as this is a life-long journey—the amount of time it takes to see the imbalance may shorten, and the ability to get back into balance may improve. I look forward to the day in my own practice when I can see an imbalance arising and make an adjustment before it occurs, rather than reacting and adjusting afterwards.

CREATE A SIMPLE PLAN

Now that you have a better understanding of where you would like to be in terms of balance, compared to where you are currently, create a simple plan to have just a little more balance in your life.

The following table provides an example of a simple plan for one leader. It includes one area of life in which this leader would like to have more balance, the benefit of a change, a belief they would need to shift to support this change, an action required, the support needed from others, and the conversations required as well:

Area of life for more balance/ What the benefit will be:
More time for me to rest (as work consists of back-to-back meetings and we have 2 kids). Benefit—I'll be more effective as a boss and a parent as I'll have more perspective and feel less resentful.
Belief I'll need to shift:
That time to care for myself is important. Also, that I value myself enough to book the time and follow through in order to keep the promise to myself.
Action:
Book 1.5 hours a week to go for a walk in the forest on my own (or go for coffee, or to the spa, etc.)
Support needed:
Someone to take the kids so I can keep my commitment to myself.
Conversations needed:
• Set a boundary for meetings—instead of 60 minutes with no breaks in between, make them 45 minutes with a 10 minute break. • Ask my partner to support me when I want to let go of this promise to myself. • Ask my partner how I can support her in booking time for herself as well.

NEXT STEPS:

Gather all of the information you have developed, in all of the steps so far, and take the time to reflect on what the awakening is for you, and what the implications are for your leadership and your life.

STEP #7
REFLECT ON THE AWAKENING AND
IMPLICATIONS FOR YOUR LEADERSHIP

Take the time now to sit with the new information you have gathered about yourself and what is important to you at this point in your leadership and your life. Stepping back to reflect on this will create the next awakening needed to take your authenticity to the next level.

An awakening occurs when you learn something new about yourself that is startlingly different than what you believe to be true.

EXERCISE TO UNDERSTAND YOUR AWAKENING:

Reflect on your what you've learned about your Authentic Self, values, purpose, leadership principles, life vision and work-life balance assessment. Next, using the following questions for self reflection, as well as the action worksheet included in Appendix A - understand and articulate your awakening.

1. What are you learning about your life and how you would like to live, aligned with Authentic Self? What are you becoming awake to?

2. How important is what you are learning about yourself? What about it makes it important to you?

3. What are you learning about your leadership and how you would like to bring your Authentic Self into your day-to-day activities?

4. What are the implications for you leadership? What will you focus on for the next 3 months? For the next 12 months?

5. What are two strengths that will support you as you move forward?

6. What are two self-limiting beliefs that it will be helpful to shift or let go of, in order for you to move forward? How can you reframe these to improve your leadership?

7. Is there any support you would need to have in order to be more authentic in your leadership?

NEXT STEPS:

Take your new awakening and understanding of the implications for your leadership and your life, and complete the next steps—setting goals and creating your inner development plan—both will help you to move forward in ways that support your Authentic Leadership.

STEP #8
SET YOUR GOALS

TO SET GOALS OR NOT?

One way to live authentically is to become aware, live in the moment, and allow what will come to come.

Another is to create the life you want.

Neither is better or worse, they are merely different. This book shares the path for you as an authentic leader to take action to achieve your life vision. The actions you take that are congruent with your life vision and Authentic Self align you in each moment with your personal truth. When you are also aligned with organizational goals, you create a win, win, win situation for all.

In addition, for those who set goals, some would rather set a more general intention rather than a specific goal with a target. Intentions are more general and set the tone and provide a theme for the next time period.

Examples of goals include:

- Career/Business—Increase gross sales to $5M annually by December.
- Personal Development—Find a community of support by September and attend 6 group sessions by December.
- Health—practice yoga 2-3 times per week for an hour—have a consistent practice by May.

Examples of intentions are:

- Career/business—to improve sales by cultivating exceptional customer experiences
- Personal development—find a community and practice accepting support
- Health—to create the conditions for a renewed sense of strength and wellness

As an authentic leader you may set goals (or intentions) on an ongoing basis, for both a) the external parts of your life (i.e. work, education, family) as well as b) your personal inner development (i.e. Awareness and letting go of control, rebalancing the voice of the inner critic, etc.). Inner development is foundational to amplifying your strengths, reframing limiting beliefs, and creating new, helpful habits, all of which will support realizing your external goals.

There are many goal-setting systems for leaders inside and outside of organizations. It has been proven time and again that when you write your goals down they are more likely to occur.

What is different about the Authentic You™ Personal Planning System is two-fold:

First, **the goals or intentions (for the experiences that occur externally to you) you set are aligned to your Authentic Self** and what is truly important to you at this point in your life (and not just who you are with limited awareness of your Authentic Self because of the unhelpful aspects of personality), and

Second, **the experiences that occur internally for you are represented as well and an inner development plan in included**. Inner development is essential to achieving your external goals. It supports leadership and life effectiveness through unfolding awareness of both your strengths and the limiting aspects of personality.

PRINCIPLES FOR GOAL-SETTING

When setting goals, it is important to remember a few basic principles:

- Make them as specific and actionable as you can.
- Give them a timeframe and a completion date when appropriate.
- Try to make them realistic and within your control while also about 10% outside your comfort zone to inspire growth.
- Have just a few so they are not overwhelming (you can set more later—you have a lifetime to practice).

Choose a time horizon (six months or a year for example) and use this as the starting point for your goals and inner development plan for now. See how this feels and adjust as you live your life.

Goal setting involves understanding where the gaps are, what your priorities are, and what actions will help to move you forward.

EXERCISE TO SET GOALS

Use the action worksheet included in Appendix A, as well as your values, purpose, life vision, and the work-life balance assessment (including any business or other goals you would like to set) and complete the following exercise:

1. Choose a time horizon that feels right for your life (i.e. one year).
2. Review the Work-life-Balance Assessment you completed, and

your reflections on the awakening created by completing all of the steps so far, and decide on the two to three areas in your life in which you would like to see something different occurring (i.e. the three areas where you are currently spending the least amount of energy. In the above example it is career, spirituality and health).

3. For each of these parts of your life set a goal that will focus your choices and actions for the next applicable timeframe. Examples of goals include:
   - Career/business: Increase gross sales to $5M annually by December.
   - Spirituality: Find a community of support by September and attend 6 group sessions by December.
   - Health: practice yoga 2 to 3 times per week for an hour—have a consistent practice by May.

   Record your goals in your Authentic You™ Personal Learning Journal™ or on the Authentic You™ Poster.

4. Decide on one action that is the next step that you can take to achieve your goals—this can be for the next day, week, month or quarter (however long you think you need to complete this step). Record these as well. Some examples are:
   - Career/Business: Implement the social networking strategy in the next month (by June).
   - Spirituality: Talk to three people whom I admire, and ask them how they include spirituality in their life (if they do) and where they find their community of support (by July).
   - Health: Sign up for a monthly package at a Yoga Studio or download a free Yoga App on my Smartphone (by April 15).

5. Review your goals on a regular basis and reflect on whether they need to be adjusted or whether you have achieved them. Make adjustments where necessary.

NEXT STEPS

Review all of the information developed so far in your Authentic You™ Personal Planning System, and complete your inner development plan.

STEP #9
CREATE YOUR INNER DEVELOPMENT PLAN

This chapter focuses on your inner development plan—first by providing context-setting concepts, and second, through practical exercises you can complete.

Your inner development plan focuses on awareness and self-managing to have more choice about the thoughts, emotions and physiological sensations you pay attention to, the guidance they provide, and the choices for your behaviours as you align them with your Authentic Self.

Creating and implementing this plan will support you to be authentic in your leadership and your life.

First let's set the context by introducing the idea of inner development as the Black Box or next frontier for leadership development.

THE BLACK BOX OF GREAT LEADERSHIP

Business consultant and author Jim Collins, in *Good to Great*[65], talks about the phenomenon of a "Level 5 Leader," someone who, through a combination of personal will and humility, takes a company from good to great—"companies that made the leap from good results to great results—averaging cumulative stock returns 6.9 times the general market"[66]—and sustained those results for at least fifteen years.

How do these leaders do it? Leaders in "good to great" companies follow several principles, including: practicing a culture of discipline; leveraging technology as a support for growth; clarifying that the service or product is aligned with passion, ability and economic need.

In addition, the person at the helm models and fosters "Level 5" leadership.

---

65   Jim Collins, *Good to Great—Why Some Companies Make the Leap... and Others Don't* (New York: HarperCollins Publishers, 2001), pp. 20 - 21.

66   Ibid, p 3.

In order to become a Level 5 leader, posits Collins, leaders must be engaged with their own inner development. Collins states:

Our research exposed Level 5 as a key component inside the black box of what it takes to shift a company from good to great. Yet inside that black box is yet another black box—namely, the inner development of a person to Level 5. We could speculate what might be inside that black box, but it would mostly be just that—speculation.[67]

Level 5 Leadershop Model*:

Level 5 Executive
(humility and will)

The "black box" of
the Inner Journey

Effective Leader

Competent Manager

Contributing Team
Member

Highly Capable
Individual

Source: "Good to Great", Jim Collins

Collins outlines the steps leaders take in their careers as they move from being a valued individual contributor, through a competent Manager and Executive, to a Level 5 Leader where the distinction is a high level of humility paired with an iron will.

While Collins prefers to leave a leader's inner development as a mystery[68], many others have ventured into that unknown terrain, creating

---

67   Ibid, p 37-38.

68   Author's note - I share the information about the Level 5 Leader to show that leaders such as Jim Collins are pondering the idea of the inner development and that this book provides our understanding of how it can occur. I am not making the claim that if you complete the steps in this book you will become a Level 5 Leader.

models, concepts and exercises that have benefitted leaders and helped them on the journey. There are many books, programs, philosophies and types of guides you could work with for your inner development. The beauty, and the challenge—as too many options can be overwhelming—is that becoming authentic requires a customized approach, and you get to choose your own path. Your choice can be guided by what you feel needs focus at a certain point in time, and what your comfort zone is for the new awareness.

This book is, in part, a distillation of concepts and exercises designed to shine the light on inner development; this chapter is focused on inner development through awareness and self-management for authenticity.

INNER DEVELOPMENT

The inner development of a leader begins with the awareness that, in addition to your external experiences, there is also an inner realm where you are having other experiences. As was introduced in detail in Chapter Six: Action, the experiences you are having internally—thoughts, emotions, physiological sensations, and intuition—are guiding your behaviours. Awareness and choice about your internal experiences support continuous improvement externally—how your leadership shows up with others.

Many leading-edge companies are becoming aware of the value of their employee's inner development and are building it into their culture. Google is a prime example as they focus on inner development for increased compassion as a strategic asset for the bottom line.

Google focuses on Inner Development

In his TED talk, Chade-Meng Tan,[69] one of the leaders at Google, discusses how compassion translates into tangible business benefits. Such benefits include increased "collaboration, initiative, and creativity" which encourage employees to naturally choose to do the right thing in every interaction. Tan then outlines the "three ingredients for practicing everyday compassion in business,"[70] the last of which emphasizes the importance of inner development.

---

69 Tan Chade-Meng, *Everyday Compassion at Google video,* posted April 2011. http://www.ted.com/talks/lang/eng/chade_meng_tan_everyday_compassion_at_google. html

70 Ibid.

Leadership development at Google focuses on strength of character with an emphasis on "self-awareness, self-mastery, empathy and compassion".[71] They have a seven week leadership program focusing on inner development, "searching inside yourself" to develop emotional intelligence, foundational to practicing compassion.

> Google's program for inner development has three components: "...**attention training** (to create a quality of mind that is calm and clear), **developing self knowledge and self mastery** (to be able to observe our thought stream and the process of emotions with high clarity, objectivity and from a third person perspective), and to **create new mental habits** (i.e. wanting each person you interact with to be happy—this is unconsciously picked up by other people and so changes everything at work as it builds trust)"[72].

COMFORT ZONE

As you take action towards authenticity, it can be helpful to get to know your current comfort zone—where you feel comfortable with any situation or task.

If you do the same activities day in and day out and stay comfortable in all that you do, you will get the same results you have gotten until now. If this is what you want, then that is okay. If, however, you are experiencing frustration or restlessness or if you've experienced an awakening, and there is the need to evolve, then it may be time for you to be okay with getting a bit uncomfortable.

A note here: it is also possible to do too much too fast—similar to how some leaders live each day—which can be counterproductive to the process. It can be helpful to discern just how much is too much. This is an important and uniquely personal question to ask yourself.

Going too far out of your comfort zone may push you over the edge and into overwhelm. Too much, and you don't learn. Too little, and you don't learn. The challenge is to proceed at a rate that is about 10% outside what you are currently comfortable with, enough to create a healthy tension so that even while you experience cognitive dissonance and discomfort, you are still able to work with it and make the needed changes.

---

71   Ibid.

72   Ibid, quotes taken directly from the video "Everyday Compassion at Google".

Again, choice comes into play.

You get to choose the right level of intensity for your inner development, given all that is going on in your life at this time.

Imagine going to the gym when you have not been there for a while, and beginning to work with a more challenging routine. You would need to gauge the right level of weights to work with so that you would have progress and not injury. The same idea applies to your inner development.

What amount or type of inner development exercise is going to take you out of your comfort zone by about 10% more than normal functioning? If it feels like too much to begin something new at this time, ask yourself if is there is an alternate method or resource that feels less intense, and/or if you should leave this issue for the time being and return to it when you feel more ready to tackle it.

For some leaders, reading a specific book—for example *Getting Our Bodies Back*[73], which is a great resource for authentic leaders—may be experienced as a 2 out of 10 in terms of stress level, where a 1 feels like a breeze and 10 feels too intense even consider. For other people, or at other times in your life, reading the same book may feel like a 9 out of 10 and too much to deal with.

It is important to honour when it is <u>not</u> the right time.

At times, you will need to put your inner development on the back burner until you have the space and energy to do the work.

Sometimes your inner development <u>is</u> simply to learn how to make the space and time to eventually do your work. You may need to first clear out the psychological space—by learning to do less, letting go of tasks, delegating and learning to let go of control—before even considering tak-

---

73   Christine Caldwell, *Getting Our Bodies Back—Recovery, Healing, and Transformation through Body-Centered Psychotherapy,* (Boston: Shambhala Publications, Inc., 1996). In her book, Caldwell provides an important overview of how habits used for calming yourself down (self soothing) can become addictions. Additions could also be defined as unhealthy habits. If you are not able to stay present to uncomfortable emotions in day-to-day life, you will continue to seek out these addictions. They can range from drinking excessive amounts of caffeine to constantly twisting your hair with your finger, to alcoholism and many others. She provides an overview of how important it is to be able to stay present through the uncomfortable emotions. This is an essential concept for self-managing. In the book, Caldwell suggests practices for letting go of these addictions. As an Authentic Leader, it is important to be open to understanding which automatic behaviours are currently addictions for you. These could be showing up as self-limiting thoughts and behaviours that are getting in the way of your Authentic Self emerging.

ing on anything new. Then you can begin to make actual space by booking time to do the self-reflection and practices needed and to create new habits.

Example: Joe is the Manager of Strategic Planning for a financial services firm. He has worked 6 days a week for 12 hours a day for the past 20 years. (Does the pace sound familiar?)

He has a strong work ethic and believes that rest is a waste of time.

Joe finds himself burned out and overwhelmed after the 20th year as well as overweight from all the travel and inattention to nutrition and wellness.

He begins to work with a coach as he is having a difficult time with guilt when taking a rest. He feels so exhausted and doesn't have the energy to do much more than the basics each day. He definitely doesn't have the desire to meet with friends or to do activities outside of work.

He visits his doctor and naturopath and discovers he has adrenal fatigue.

The coach provides him with some insight for shifting his perspective by creating an aha moment. She asks "Do you ever remember a time in your life when you did nothing?" "What would it be like for you, if you feel like doing nothing, to do nothing—until you feel like doing something?" "If doing nothing feels too daunting, what would be different for your wellness if you learned to do just a little less, more of the time?"

Joe breathes a huge sigh of relief as he experiences an aha moment and sees a new possibility for rest and less effort (without guilt).

Years later, when Joe has a much more balanced life, he still sighs when he remembers her questions and the spaciousness and relief he felt as he considered a different way than what he was used to.

When you undertake a new activity, or think about a new possibility, it can feel scary and uncomfortable. It may be different than what your current beliefs say are "ok" and safe. In order to shift these beliefs to include new information or perspectives, in order to evolve as a person, you must be willing to get a bit uncomfortable.

EXERCISES FOR INNER DEVELOPMENT

Reflect on all of the components you have completed in your Authentic You™ Personal Planning System, and identify one or two beliefs or behaviours that may be limiting your effectiveness.

In order to be authentic, it is important to let these go, or shift them, so you are able to move forward to achieve the goals and life vision you have articulated for yourself.

1. Look at your goals and identify where a limiting belief or behaviour is getting in the way.

   For Example:

   My goal: Learn how to delegate more effectively within 3 months. Limiting belief or behaviour: I am impatient with others who complete tasks differently than I would have; I judge other approaches—believing that using a different approach than I would, will not produce as good a result.

2. Think of a way to reframe the limiting belief so that you think about it in a way that is more helpful.

   Example: The shift that is required is to see delegation as essential to your effectiveness and getting things done through others as efficient rather than extra effort and stress. Remind yourself that delegating gives the other person the chance to shine and to do the tasks they love to do!

3. Once you are able to see a new way forward, think about new actions you can take to create a new habit or a behaviour that is more aligned with who you are.

   Example: If you are learning how to delegate, you may need to let go of control and trust others in ways you haven't before. It may be difficult for you to do this as you have too much on your plate and it feels quicker to complete the work yourself,

*especially when an employee brings work back that you have
asked them to do, and it has errors in it.*

Note: If, on your own, you are not able to reframe or identify actions
you can take, this may be the time to seek out support. Talk to peers, your
boss, friends, and family who you know will be supportive when you ask
for help. And if you are still not able to resolve the issue, you may want
to consider seeking targeted, short-term help from a coach, counselor or
therapist.

Next, research what exercises you can do to achieve your goal and to
create new behaviours that will support achieving it. In addition, identify
exercises you can complete for awareness and self-managing.

You may be able to develop your own exercises, and/or you may need
assistance from others. This is where the experience of a coach can be
very helpful as they understand internal experiences and how to create the
necessary shifts.

CREATE YOUR INNER DEVELOPMENT PLAN

Use the action worksheet in Appendix A as well as the examples below
to create your inner development plan.

The following table shows sample goals in an organizational context
(for situations that are frequently learning opportunities for leaders at one
time or another in their career), as well as sample actions and exercises for
your inner development plan. In addition to reviewing them as examples
for developing your own plan, consider using these exercises as the content
for your plan if they ring true for you.

Note—the timeframe for achieving most goals in this example is 3
months. Your timeframes may vary depending on how much time you need
to achieve the internal shifts required, and to create new behaviours.

MY GOAL

Your goal:
Learn how to delegate more effectively within 3 months.
Limiting belief or behaviour and mindset shift required:
Impatience with others who complete tasks differently than you would have; judging other approaches—believing that using a different approach than yours will not produce as good a result. Mindset shift required: To see delegation as essential to your effectiveness, and getting things done through others as efficient rather than an extra effort. Delegating also gives the other person the chance to shine!
Exercises to help shift or let go of it:
Each week create a list of 5 things that need to get done, who can complete them (not you), and what support you can provide so they learn. Assign the task and support the person as they complete it.
Exercises for awareness and self-managing:
Awareness – Pay attention to what happens for you (i.e. your anxiousness, lack of trust, and desire to take the work back and do it yourself) when the person completes the work differently from how you would have. Self-managing - Practice self-managing and talk to the person with a non-judgmental tone in order to check understanding; provide feedback and ask them to make the changes themselves.

Your goal:
Improve your ability to give up resources when this is the right answer for the company—within 1 week.
Limiting belief or behaviour and mindset shift required:
Blaming peers in other departments for getting resources that you wanted to acquire for your own projects. Mindset shift required—Doing the right thing for the customer and company is essential. Use the company vision and values as a starting point for working together; collaboration between departments is the key.
Exercises to help shift or let go of it:
In your resource allocation meeting, practice giving up one thing that is low risk for your team.
Exercises for awareness and self-managing:
Awareness – Pay attention to the process—what occurs in your mind. The process of blaming may arise in this discussion. The content may be blaming because you believe the person doesn't value you and you judge yourself as weak if you give up any resources. Self-managing – Notice what happens for you internally when you give up the resource, and what the reaction is of the person you give it to. Reflect on the benefits for the team and the company. Debrief this experience with your supervisor and do one thing personally to celebrate your willingness to shift.

Your goal:
Be a more effective manager—within 3 months.
Limiting belief or behaviour and mindset shift required:
Getting defensive when people disagree with you or challenge your assumptions. Mindset shift required—Realizing you are doing something right to create a great environment in which people feel safe enough to share their opinions, particularly when they may cause disagreement. Thank them for challenging you.
Exercises to help shift or let go of it:
In 1:1 and group interactions, encourage team members to disagree with you and to challenge your assumptions in order to ensure that you have more complete information for decision making.
Exercises for awareness and self-managing:
Awareness - Pay attention to what happens in your body (thoughts, emotions) when others challenge you. Using *The Wisdom of the Enneagram* book, review the Levels of Development for your personality type, to understand what your healthy levels look like, and review the exercises suggested for when your type is under stress. Reflect on what your automatic pattern is. Self-managing – Practice deepening your breathing and staying open to hearing what other people have to say. Watch your tone and body language as you respond. Practice letting go of judgments as they arise and ask questions to clarify your understanding.

Your goal:
Improve your communication skills in difficult or uncomfortable situations—within 3 months.
Limiting belief or behaviour and mindset shift required:
Avoiding difficult conversations and/or being unaware of their impact on others.
Mindset shift required—Difficult conversations are opportunities to strengthen a relationship; they get less difficult with practice.
Exercises to help shift or let go of it:
Practice clearing issues within 24 hours of when they occur, so they don't become big issues.
Exercises for awareness and self-managing:
Awareness - Pay attention to your current pattern and how you think about clearing issues. (Do you avoid them at all cost? Do you get angry and defensive and show it in your tone and body language?
Self-managing - Practice using the arc of intense energy model to breathe and stay present through the conversation while you clear the issue.

Your goal:
Improve your healthy debating skills in Leadership Team meetings on highly contentious strategic issues—within 3 months.
Limiting belief or behaviour and mindset shift required:
A fear of debating; seeing it as aggressive Mindset shift required—As an introvert, you can learn to enjoy debating as a kind of healthy sparring to come up with the best solution—just keep it focused on ideas rather than people.
Exercises to help shift or let go of it:
In each team meeting, prepare prior to the meeting and write down ideas for questions. Ask three questions and then state your opinion.
Exercises for awareness and self-managing:
Awareness - Notice what occurs for you in your body when you interact with team members. Notice your assumptions about their reactions and practice staying present through uncomfortable feelings that may arise. Self-managing - Practice deep breathing and relaxing as you continue to engage in the conversation. After the meeting reflect on one thing you did well and one thing you could have done differently. Incorporate these learnings in the next team meeting.

Your goal:
Practice focus and discipline for more effective time management—within 3 months.
Limiting belief or behaviour and mindset shift required:
Avoiding planning; not thinking strategically.

Mindset shift required—Ongoing time to step back to see the forest, will allow you to be more effective when you go back into the day-to-day of walking amongst the trees. |
| **Exercises to help shift or let go of it:** |
| Using your Authentic You™ Personal Planning System (particularly your purpose and life vision) as context, once each quarter, practice prioritizing and planning for the next month, quarter and the balance of the year. |
| **Exercises for awareness and self-managing:** |
| Awareness - Pay attention to how you think about planning and whether you value it or not. If you do not value it, practice thinking about it in a different way—in a way that allows you to be enthusiastic about, it or at the least accept that planning will support you to be more effective. Before doing the planning exercise, reflect on how you can do it, and where, so that it aligns with your purpose and life vision (i.e. you can do it on a weekend away, or you can make your favorite meal as a celebration once it is complete). Reflect on how you currently plan, and how it would feel if it you did it in a way that is aligned with your authentic self.

Self-managing – When you are planning and you notice discomfort, practice self-managing to be aware of what is coming up for you. Reflect on what is behind the discomfort and what you are learning about yourself as a result. |

NEXT STEPS

Now that you have created your inner development plan, you have completed all nine steps of your Authentic You™ Personal Planning System. The next step is to reflect on each step and make any adjustments before you put them into practice on an ongoing basis.

CHAPTER NINE:
PUTTING THE AUTHENTIC YOU™ PERSONAL PLANNING SYSTEM INTO PRACTICE

Constant review and attention will bring your dreams to life.

USING THE SYSTEM FOR THE REST OF YOUR LIFE

Now that you have your first iteration of the Authentic You™ Personal Planning System completed, what do you do with it?

This system is helpful both the first time you use it for gaining personal clarity, as well as on an ongoing basis for the rest of your life. It is meant to provide the foundation for your inner guidance system to help you constantly recalibrate your orientation to living as your Authentic Self. This is especially helpful in a world of ambiguity and change where staying true to yourself is the essential, and sometimes more difficult, path.

After completing the system for the first time, you can review and revise your answers whenever you like. The timing for these reviews may be different for you than for others. You get to choose the pace. You may find it helpful to revisit your Authentic You™ Personal Planning System on a regular basis (monthly or annually), and/or whenever the need arises. For some, an annual review is helpful, for others they simply wait until the next time that feels right arises.

If you have the opportunity to integrate the system, into your career planning and performance management conversations, an annual review fits with these organizational processes. To honor your authenticity, though, it is recommended that you choose a review option that is aligned with your values and goals, and pay attention to how the timing feels. This may or may not coincide with your organization's schedule. If it feels out of alignment with your Authentic Self—too rushed or not frequent enough—simply choose a different pace. Remember, you have creative control of your life!

What follow are some possible review options for timing and process – Annual, Short-term (monthly and quarterly) and Ongoing.

ANNUAL REVIEW

The first way to use the Authentic You™ Personal Planning System is annually in a holistic review. Each year you will want to check in and validate each of the components.

Some of the components may remain largely the same (values, purpose, leadership principles, life vision), and others may change substantially (life vision, work-life balance, goals, inner development plan). If there are no changes to the elements, just reviewing them will provide an opportunity to deepen your understanding of what you want to create for the next steps in your life.

SHORT-TERM REVIEWS (MONTHLY OR QUARTERLY)

In addition to the annual reviews and course corrections, it is also helpful to review your progress and make adjustments on a monthly or quarterly basis. It can be helpful to review the more immediate elements including work-life balance assessment, goals, and inner development plan in the context of any changes you may make to the other components or any awakenings you may have experienced.

Your work-life balance may be better some months than others. There may be times when you are noticing that you are particularly off balance— for example you are completing an MBA while working and having a family, or you have just received a promotion and doubled the size of your team to 5,000 people with 20 Direct Reports, or you have just accepted a position on a Board of Directors for a nonprofit organization. All of these kinds of events can cause an imbalance that requires course correcting in order to maintain a strong foundation of personal wellness.

Goals are similar. Business as well as personal goals may require adjusting monthly or quarterly, although you may not adjust them using the same schedule.

Regarding your inner development plan—if you think of your personality as an onion—with an endless number of layers to your unfolding authenticity—you can see the need for course correction as you get through one layer and develop awareness of the next. For example, a first step on your journey to being an authentic leader may be to slow your body to become aware of the pace at which your mind is racing and of all the unhelpful thoughts that are occurring. You may need to make space in your life for inner development. When you are burned out, if you have ever experienced this, you may not have the capacity for even a small change in your behavior or way of thinking—even if it is just to learn to take care of yourself more. Once you have worked through this block by completing exercises with a coach or community of support, and integrating the willingness to care about yourself first, back into your life, then you may experience the next level of awareness, or layer of who you are, as it shows up.

Your next step may be to learn to set boundaries and to say 'no' in the face of many requests for you to take on more and more accountability.... And next may be to build your capacity to stay present with intensely uncomfortable feelings... and so on.

There will always be more layers.

When you return to your Authentic You™ Personal Learning Journal, Authentic You™ Poster and life-vision board over the years, and review each of the components, you may feel recharged. You may have just a bit more hope and trust that you are living your life in ways that bring you joy. You will then have an increased capacity to stay the course, even on the days when you are tired and frustrated. You will have a clear, inner guidance system for your journey and you will be able open to the unknown and continue to put one foot in front of the next as an authentic leader.

ONGOING REVIEWS

For your personal use,[74] the following are suggestions for other ways you can use the planning system on an ongoing basis:
- Spend time reviewing it and exploring how it feels when you remember who you are when at your best and what is truly important to you at this point in your life.

---

74 At the organizational level, the Authentic You™ Personal Planning System can be "hardwired" into management processes in order to improve business results through individual growth and development. As each individual is able to stand in their authenticity, so the organization feels the impact as it becomes more authentic as well.

- Share it with your supervisor as an opportunity for relationship building, and for them to be able to support you bringing your Authentic Self into your work.
- Revisit the goals and inner development plan on a regular basis as a part of your performance management process; integrate them into your personal objectives and career development plan.
- When you are at a point of transition or a major life-change occurs, revisit the entire system as a way to re-orient yourself when that awakening has shaken you to the core.
- Evolve the different components as you gain more information about your Authentic Self, or as you discover different ways that you want to contribute as a leader.
- Use it to make decisions on a day-to day basis when the situation is unclear and the future uncertain.

CELEBRATION OF PROGRESS

Many of you may discover that your inner critic focuses on the lack of results and progress in your life. You can manage your inner critic by being intentional about recognizing and reflecting on results. This can be done in your Authentic You™ Personal Learning Journal. You can also have a separate book specifically for celebrations where you recognize your progress. You could also involve others. The important thing is that you replace the negative voice of the inner critic with a more balanced and compassionate voice that can see the progress being made—even when moving forward requires taking a direction you were not thinking you would take.

Remember that progress is not always linear. When you are a continuous learner, you can begin to see the rest of your life as a practice for being an authentic leader and authentic person. As a continuous learner, you will have so much more patience for the idea of baby steps, and so much more compassion for mistakes. In fact, you will start to see mistakes or distractions as a gift—a necessary, and even welcomed, part of the journey.

WHO IS IN YOUR COMMUNITY OF SUPPORT?

The world is longing for community. This deep-rooted desire is showing up in the social networking world through the massive numbers of people connecting virtually via Facebook, Linked In, Twitter, Ning, etc. There is a similar longing for community within organizations, and yet many leaders tend to isolate as they feel the need to "figure it out by themselves." A leader may be in relationship with many in order to conduct business and yet, at the same time, they may have very few people to whom they are able, or feel safe enough, to show their Authentic Self.

Authentic leaders spend time with other authentic leaders. They build a community of support, finding ways to help and be helped by others who are also living as their authentic selves. Participating in such a community can give you what I call an "Authenticity Recharge™." Authenticity Recharges™ are facilitated sessions that occur on a regular basis where a group of participants gather to check in on their progress and receive support for their practice of being Authentic. These are called recharges as a person can come into them, get recharged, discover new practices, and feel more hopeful as they re-enter their day to day lives.

Authenticity Recharges™ provide leaders with a place to practice being vulnerable with others in order to develop their capacity to stay authentic in situations where it would be easier to go with the flow and forfeit what is important to them. Such support is helpful as leaders experience their next learning opportunity, or find themselves in situations such as spending time with family, or with other people whose behaviours may trigger them. With ongoing support leaders can learn to work through their own triggers and hear the experiences of others in similar situations.

This is often one of the most difficult steps for leaders on the journey to authenticity. As you open to being supported, you may feel vulnerable and exposed, which can be scary. Paradoxically, as you learn to be appropriately vulnerable with others you will also experience your power. Others will experience you as approachable and empathetic, (particularly when they put themselves at risk by challenging your assumptions or disagreeing with you) and they in turn can feel safe enough to be their authentic selves. This can lead to a huge awakening and shift that allows you, for what may be the first time, to experience meaningful relationships that you may have longed for yet haven't allowed yourself to be in.

Two ways of experiencing a community of support for your own Authenticity Recharge™ are by engaging in peer mentoring and/or a personal board of directors.

PEER MENTORING

Peer mentoring involves a community of people who come together, either one-on-one or in a group to provide support and feedback. They meet on an ongoing basis for a common purpose. If one-on-one, they meet to provide mutual support and feedback on specific topics that are challenging at that time. If in a group, these sessions may be led by the peers or by an experienced facilitator.

A peer-mentoring group can take many forms and levels of structure depending on the needs and wants of the participants. These groups are helpful to monitor progress and to provide a safe place to practice and strengthen your authenticity. Once you have spent time with your peer-mentoring group, you will leave the space with a little more capacity for authenticity in a world where this is not always the norm. You will also gain hope and validation for your unique way of leading.

The level of support and connection, as well as the empathy and compassion, that grows from a group with a common purpose and language can be quite profound. It is a wonderful feeling to realize that there are others on a similar path to living authentically—you are not alone.

A PERSONAL BOARD OF DIRECTORS

A Personal Board of Directors or a Dream Team, as it is also called, is a group of people whom you can call upon at times, over the years, for your personal support. This might include others whom you respect and admire and who are more experienced in an area you would like to understand, or a business or health professional whose support you draw on from time to time, or a family member you can seek out for advice and guidance. Some examples include an executive with experience building the business you are in, a retired executive whom you set up a formal mentoring arrangement with, a yoga instructor, a dentist, family doctor, naturopath, personal trainer, your best friend, or others including a coach, counselor or therapist.

EXERCISES

Use the action worksheet included in Appendix A and choose the exercises that feel right for you to put what you have learned into practice:

1. Decide on how often you will review your Authentic You™ Personal Planning System and Authentic You™ Personal Learning Journal: monthly, quarterly, annually, or some other regular interval that works for you. Complete the reviews, making changes when you would like to shift your current work-life balance, or set a different goal.

2. As you revisit the Steps and make changes to evolve each component (Authentic Self, values, etc.), reflect on how these changes feel. Notice what you are learning about yourself, and share what you've learned with someone in your community of support.

3. In addition to the regular intervals, when you are at a crossroads in your life or career, or when a major life event has occurred, and when it feels like the right time, review all the components of your Authentic You™ Personal Planning System and make adjustments where required. Notice how your choices and actions take on a new focus as a result.

4. Share the changes with family and friends and members of your community of support.

CHAPTER TEN
TRUTH, CONSCIOUSNESS AND AUTHENTICITY

Never underestimate the ripple effect you have as an authentic leader.

As you model authenticity, you will have an impact on others. You may plant a seed of possibility for them to live life as their true selves, and it can change their lives.

As you become authentic, the ripple moves outward from you in every moment.

When others experience your way of being, they may experience an awakening. For some, the timing will be right for them and they will heed it and take action immediately. For others it may not ever take hold; and for others still it may simply take time to germinate. If and when they heed their wake-up call, authenticity's gift of choice, personal clarity and inner peace (more of the time) will be passed on to countless others in their lives as well.

AUTHENTICITY ON A GLOBAL SCALE
The larger context for this book is the science and philosophy of the ripple effect. Being authentic has implications that are far-reaching and significant. In order to understand them it is helpful to understand how authentic leaders, by making powerful or life-affirming choices, can impact consciousness and peace on a global scale.

Authenticity means making life-affirming choices more of the time.

Over the years, it has become consistently evident that when a person completes the Authentic You™ Personal Planning System, they reconnect with their unique way to help make the world a better place. They also choose positivity and optimism more of the time. When you are authentic, your behaviours and beliefs stem from a deep personal conviction and knowledge of truth and the right thing to do. In other words, by being more authentic you are practicing living at higher levels of consciousness, which I will discuss shortly. When self-managing, authentic leaders pay attention to all three sources of intelligence (the head, heart, and body—including intuition), to tap into the database of what some call a collective consciousness, choosing responses aligned with a universal truth.

In addition, the Authentic You™ Personal Planning System helps you to develop the personal clarity about what choices are life-affirming for you, to cultivate the ability to listen to all three sources of intelligence, and by doing so, to tap into your intuition, or the collective consciousness for making decisions.

So what is consciousness? What is the collective consciousness? How do we know what is truth?

MUSCLE TESTING AND CONSCIOUSNESS

In addressing these questions, it can be helpful to look at David R. Hawkins' research on consciousness and the basis of behaviour, and the implications of this research for authenticity. In *Power vs Force*[75] Hawkins distinguishes between power (making life-affirming choices for the good of all) and force (making life-destructing choices that impact others negatively). He discusses how through years of extensive scientific studies of kinesiology, he discovered how muscle testing can be used to tap into universal truth (or collective consciousness) and how this supports people to tap into their power and make life-affirming decisions.

In muscle testing, a person undergoes a simple test in which they are given a true-or-false statement ("It is healthy for me to eat sugar at this time"; or, "I am meant to take this job opportunity at this time," etc.). As the practitioner (or the person themselves) makes this statement, their muscles are tested by simple means (pressing down on an outstretched arm, for

---

75   David R. Hawkins, M.D., Ph.D., *Power vs Force, The Hidden Determinants of Human Behaviour.* 3rd ed (Carlsbad, CA: Hay House, Inc. (Originally published in Sedona, Ariz.: Veritas Publishing), 2002), pp 132 - 141.

example). The person's physical response will show up as either weak or strong. When a statement tests strong it means that it is true on a universal scale—it is healthy and life-affirming. When a statement tests weak, it is false, meaning life-destructing or not in alignment with the person's (and the universal) truth.

Authentic leaders make life-affirming choices based on the inner guidance, tapping into universal truth through their ability to override their personality and listen to their Authentic Self. Authenticity fosters a realization of true power unfettered by the ideas of the personality or ego. Over time, the use of force comes into play less and less.

The ability to tap into this universal truth forms the basis for Hawkins' book. He writes:

> The individual human mind is like a computer terminal connected to a giant database. The database is human consciousness itself, of which our own cognizance is merely an individual expression, but with its roots in the common consciousness of all mankind. This database is the realm of genius; because to be human is to participate in the database, everyone by virtue of his birth, has access to genius. The unlimited information contained in the database has now been shown to be readily available to anyone in a few seconds, at anytime and in any place. This is indeed an astonishing discovery, bearing the power to change lives, both individually and collectively, to a degree never yet anticipated.[76]

While muscle testing is one way to access this database, being authentic is another. When leaders tap into their authenticity, they draw from a global, ethical viewpoint for making decisions. When they override personality and act from their Authentic Self, they make positive choices—for themselves, for others, and ultimately for the world. And this raises the level of collective consciousness.

As evidence of this, it is important to discuss Hawkins' Map of Consciousness and how testing weak, corresponds to levels below 200 and testing strong calibrates to over 200. What does this mean?

Hawkins has created a way of measuring consciousness—a map that is based on a numerical scale from 0—1000. The map describes levels that, "...correlate with specific processes of consciousness—emotions, percep-

---

76   Ibid, p 34—35.

tions, or attitudes, world views and spiritual beliefs."[77] The scale on the map is logarithmic meaning that "the level 300 is not twice the amplitude of 150; it is 10 to the 300th power (10^{300}). An increase of even a few points represents a major advance in power (life-affirming choices); the rate of increase in power as we move up the scale is enormous".[78] See the table below:[79]

Level of Consciousness	Level Description:	Life View	Emotion
700—1000	Enlightenment	Is	Ineffable
600	Peace	Perfect	Bliss
540	Joy	Complete	Serenity
500	Love	Benign	Reverence
400	Reason	Meaningful	Understanding
350	Acceptance	Harmonious	Forgiveness
310	Willingness	Hopeful	Optimism
250	Neutrality	Satisfactory	Trust
200	Courage	Feasible	Affirmation
175	Pride	Demanding	Scorn
150	Anger	Antagonistic	Hate
125	Desire	Disappointing	Craving
100	Fear	Frightening	Anxiety
75	Grief	Tragic	Regret
50	Apathy	Hopeless	Despair
30	Guilt	Evil	Blame
20	Shame	Miserable	Humiliation

Hawkins has found that there are two critical levels in the map of consciousness: 200 (the level associated with integrity and courage) and 500 (associated with love). The level 200 is the "fulcrum point" for power and

77 Ibid, p 67.

78 Ibid, p 75.

79 Ibid, p 68-69 (the table is partially provided here, see Hawkins' book for the complete table).

force—the difference between making life-affirming and life-destructing choices. He states that when testing for calibration,

> [A]ll attitudes, thoughts, feelings, associations, entities or historical figures, below the level of 200 make a person go weak. Everything below 200 is focused on survival; at 200 the well being of others becomes increasingly important[80]. [...] Those that calibrate higher make a person go strong. This is the balance point between weak and strong attractors, between negative and positive influence.[81]

At the level of 500 "the capacity to discern essence becomes predominant[82].

Essence, as you may remember from Chapter One, is the equivalent of Authentic Self. Hawkins goes on to state that at 500, "Love focuses on the goodness of life in all of its expressions and augments that which is positive—it dissolves negativity by recontextualizing it, rather than by attacking it.[83]

As you become authentic, it is possible to move up the levels. By modeling authenticity, you support others to do the same, thereby having a positive ripple effect on the consciousness of the world.

THE RIPPLE EFFECT

As being authentic becomes a life-long practice, you realize more of your full potential. In addition, you not only personally move up the scale of energetic calibration,[84] you support others to do the same.

> In this interconnected universe, every improvement we make in our private world improves the world at large for everyone. We all float on the collective level of consciousness of mankind so that any increment we add comes back to us. We all add to our com-

---

80   Ibid, p 70.

81   Ibid.

82   Ibid, p 90.

83   Ibid, p 91.

84   Ibid, p 68—69.

mon buoyancy by our efforts to benefit life. What we do to serve life automatically benefits all of us because we're all included in that which is life. We are life. It's a scientific fact that "what is good for you is good for me. [...] Simple kindness to one's self and all that lives is the most powerful transformational force of all.[85]

When you live and lead authentically, you have a positive ripple effect on the world. One person who has done their personal "work", who lives authentically more of the time, and who lives at a higher level on the map of consciousness, can offset millions at lower levels of consciousness.

You can do your part to support peace and collective growth in the world, just by doing your own work to become authentic—being open to awakenings as they occur, cultivating awareness, taking action aligned with Authentic Self, and opening to the next level of awareness as it arises.

SUMMARY

Never underestimate the ripple effect you have as an authentic leader.

Authentic leaders, by making powerful or life-affirming choices, can impact consciousness and peace on a global scale. In his book *Power vs Force* David R. Hawkins distinguishes between power (making life-affirming choices for the good of all) and force (making life-destructing choices that impact others negatively). He discusses how through years of extensive scientific studies of kinesiology, he discovered how muscle testing can be used to tap into universal truth, or collective consciousness and how this supports individuals to tap into their power as they make life-affirming decisions. As being authentic becomes a life-long practice, you will realize more of your full potential and impact others as you model authenticity. In addition, you not only personally move up the scale of energetic calibration on Hawkins' map of consciousness, you support the universe to move up as well.

---

85   Ibid, p 128.

AFTERWORD: MY JOURNEY

At this point in the book, and to share the context from which it has emerged, I would like to share my life journey with you. First I will describe my external journey, and second my inner development. While this is only one person's journey to authenticity, and each person's is different, I hope this story will be an inspiration for you as you begin your own.

MY EXTERNAL JOURNEY

I was born in Revelstoke B.C., Canada in 1962. By 1991, at the age of 29, I was the owner of a women's clothing store called "Tana Lee". I loved the business—spending time with clients, buying clothing hand-picked for them, enjoying the relationships, making the decisions, reaping the rewards. But I was unsettled. I was recently divorced, I had never completed my university education, I was unhappy in my personal relationships—I wanted an extraordinary life and I didn't know how to get it for myself.

So I began my personal development journey. I wasn't sure what kinds of resources were out there, so I tried out a few to see what felt right for me. I worked with a counselor, and read books, including Stephen Covey's *Seven Habits of Highly Successful People*. I remember giving the first copy away as I wasn't ready for it, and then a few years later picking it up again and devouring it—it is still one of my favorite resources. I listened to personal development tapes, talked to people who inspired me, and set goals for myself for the first time in my life.

I remember working on building my competency around public speaking—I was terrified! I joined Toastmasters, and during one of the exercises we had to talk for 2 minutes about a random topic to get used to standing up spontaneously in front of the crowd. I was asked to "Describe a snowflake," and I remember spending the longest, most uncomfortable two minutes in my life. I quit shortly afterwards. And then a year of so later, I rejoined and moved through the ranks, from participant to member of the executive, and finally local chapter President.

One goal I identified for myself at that time was to complete a Masters in Business Administration degree by 1997. I had no idea how I would do this, particularly since I had quit university the first time around—two weeks into the final (fourth) year of my undergraduate degree—and had no plans to go back to complete it. I didn't even know if the university would let me back in since it was such a long time ago. In addition, I was living in Revelstoke, working six days a week in my clothing store, and doing the books on the seventh.

I just knew I was going to do it—somehow.

I also knew I loved business and that I wanted to be a CEO. Why a CEO, I have no idea—may as well go for the top, was my motto of the day.

Regarding my personal relationships, I remember being given one of the best pieces of advice I've ever had—that I needed to give myself the life I wanted, and treat myself as I expected others to treat me (with respect), and then others would treat me the same way. I realized later this also meant that I could have an extraordinary life—single or otherwise.

Once I'd thought about my values (for the first time), set some goals, and had more of an idea where I was headed, opportunities seemed to magically appear. One day I was approached by two women who wanted to buy my clothing store, so I sold. I took a trip to Vancouver and got a job in the fashion industry there. I got promoted and ended up managing Fairweather's flagship downtown location—$3M in annual sales, a 10,000-unit inventory, and thirty-five employees on the team.

Then in 1993, again I felt unsettled. I discovered that fashion and store operations wasn't where I was meant to be—10,000 units in, and 10,000 units out, hourly targets and folding sweaters—thousands of them. Coaching staff, making targets and folding sweaters—that was my life—all in an underground mall.

I wanted something different.

The saving grace was my team. I learned so much from my relationships with them, and I am still so grateful. I learned how to support others in their development, to be successful when I was able to be myself with them, and how to take care of myself so I didn't get walked all over by my peers or my staff.

But I was unhappy. I had a bad attitude, and a great boss. She sat me down in February of 1993 and said, "We think you have a future here, but you're going to have to change a few things..." What an awakening. I hated hearing it and I needed to hear it. Thank goodness she didn't just fire me on the spot; she saw my potential.

It was a turning point for me as I realized that I could choose. I could have a positive attitude or a negative one. It was my choice. Stay or leave, it was my choice! So I scraped up every extra cent I had and invested it in an Executive Development program—mentoring, reviewing job descriptions, informational interviews, psychometric assessments to help determine what I loved. I was lost and didn't know where I was headed.

I needed to surmount a number of challenges:

- I needed to go back to school (12 years after I had quit) and complete my undergrad in order to move forward.
- I also had to get my marks up—fast—in order to be considered for the post-graduate program.
- I had to be accepted in to an MBA program,
- Figure out how in the world I was going to finance it (about $22,000 for the 2 years which seems small compared to the current price tags, and was enormous for me at that time) on a retail store manager's salary ($45,000 plus a bit of a bonus), and how I was going to complete it while working full time.
- Successfully pass the GMAT test (which I failed two times and finally after the help of a tutor passed the third time—third time a charm?).
- And then if I got accepted, I had to actually successfully complete the two-year MBA program. And believe me, I wasn't a "numbers" person, and I knew that calculus, operations research and finance would be a big part of the challenge.

Somehow I overcame each obstacle and began the Simon Fraser University Executive MBA Program in 1995. A few months into the program I walked out of a calculus refresher course (refresher? I never took it the first time), went into the bathroom, sat on the floor in the stall and cried—Who was I to think I could do this? What was I doing there? I mean really!—I had no idea just how strong my inner critic was at that time, or even that I had one.

And then I said to myself—just go back in, keep taking notes, go to all the group tutorials, keep talking to others—and at some point the light will go on and you'll understand it. I knew that somehow I would.

And I did.

In April, 1997 I finished my MBA. I more than doubled my salary as soon as I walked out of the mall for the last time. The MBA provided me with new concepts to draw upon in my business and leadership "tool box", a new level of guarded confidence, and a new community of friends and colleagues. It also helped open doors that would never otherwise have opened.

I began an eight-year adventure with BC Hydro, a Canadian government owned, multi-billion dollar hydro-electric utility. During these years I had the privilege of working in several positions, ranging from project manager for a multi-year, company-wide strategy implementation project (which by the way was both one of my huge accomplishments as well as one of my great failures. Thank goodness for those—how much we learn and how humbling they are.), to assisting the Chief Financial Officer from a strategic perspective, and ultimately to participating as a member of the Executive team.

During that eight year period, I left and returned to the company several times. One time, I moved to Chicago and worked for a world-renowned consulting firm called the Balanced Scorecard Collaborative. They were located outside of Boston, and my clients spanned the US—an energy company in New Orleans and a medical system in Duluth, Minnesota. I managed to see the Institute of Art in Chicago on the few weekends I was actually there, but mainly my life consisted of Monday mornings heading to the airport and Thursday evenings heading home from a client site.

There were lots of storms in the mid-west that year. I remember being stuck in overnight airports more than a few times—along with the many other members of the consulting subculture (who lived by the laptop and cell phone in their virtual airport offices). As I waited for planes I realized for the first time that I was satisfied with nothing—nothing could happen fast enough. I was frustrated constantly and I drove myself harder and harder. Upon reflection, I was probably burned out at the beginning of the move to the US, and by the end of six months of heavy travel (the busiest week involved eight flights), I was definitely burned out.

I remember having a conversation with my dad and he said "You know, you can get off that ladder that you are climbing. Where are you climbing to anyway?"

I quit my job in the US and moved back to Vancouver and BC Hydro in June of 2000.

And thank goodness I did. I met Chris, the man of my dreams, in 2001 and we have an extraordinary life together—we travel, spend time with our friends and family, enjoy our cat Buddy, and our dream home in downtown Vancouver.

In 2005, when I was on the executive team at BC Hydro, the career question came back up for me. How much harder did I want to work? How many more hours and groups did I have the capacity to take on? Did I really want to pursue a senior executive position?

I was burned out a second time and realized that I was letting my ego drive the bus. I was getting my self-esteem from my job instead of from just being me. And for the first time in my life, the wake-up call was loud enough. I had vertigo—I felt like I was on a boat all of the time, and believe me I'm a landlubber. I had a hormonal imbalance and adrenal fatigue.

The way I was living my life wasn't working for me anymore. It was time for a major life change.

In April, 2005 I began to get clear on my purpose (what I was intended for on this earth). I was in counseling to understand and overcome old behaviors and attitudes that were continuing to limit me, and I had just read a book by Dr. Wayne Dyer called *The Power of Intention*.

It came to me suddenly one day while I was doing yoga—I want to be a source for others who want to live their lives in ways that they realize their full potential.

And I wanted to do this with leaders in the business world. I wanted to be a guide for others to be intentional about their personal journey. And I wanted to be a conduit for other programs and resources—there are so many wonderful ones out there. I wanted to let others know what I had learned so they could navigate their own paths and design their own personal discovery program. I wanted to help them start on their path to authenticity as soon as possible and improve the quality of their lives for the rest of their journey. It would be my way to support peace, and to alleviate pain and suffering in the world.

These were my new mantras.

So I gave a year's notice and started to think about my business. My old pattern was to get busy and write a plan, get into my head and sort out the business model. So this time I spent almost two years researching, trying out new things, and processing before I started to plan. I wanted to let life unfold and to see the direction more clearly before I set it down on paper.

I began a year-long professional coaching program with New Ventures West in San Francisco and when I entered the classroom for the first time it felt like I had come home. I discovered others who were on the same path and I was blessed with a new community of support.

And out of this, Authentic Leadership Global, Inc. was born.

MY INNER DEVELOPMENT

The Guest House

This being human is a guest house.
Every morning a new arrival.

A joy, a depression, a meanness,
some momentary awareness comes
as an unexpected visitor.

Welcome and entertain them all!
Even if they're a crowd of sorrows,
who violently sweep your house
empty of its furniture,
still, treat each guest honorably.
He may be clearing you out
for some new delight.

The dark thought, the shame, the malice,
meet them at the door laughing,
and invite them in.

Be grateful for whoever comes,
because each has been sent
as a guide from beyond.

    –Rumi[86]

---

86   "The Guest House", by Rumi as shared by my teacher Sarita Chawla, Professional
Coach Course, New Ventures West, 2005.

I have been searching my entire life for inner peace and where I fit. I felt like an outsider for many years. In elementary school I was the good girl and the smart one and I remember in grade three, playing dumb at math to get attention from the teacher. And so it began.

I was the rebel in high school—lots of boyfriends and partying and testing my limits with my parents. I realize now that I hated myself and I was getting my self-esteem at that time from men. I believed that if I had a boyfriend, or if men liked me that I was okay and had value. I could feel good about myself…for that moment anyway.

I got married for the first time in 1986, when I was 24 and was divorced by 1988. As I neared my divorce I was partying way too much. On Friday nights I'd drink double martinis until the week was washed away. I was working with a counselor who believed I might be an alcoholic—I had gone into a session hung-over and told her about it.

"You need to go to a treatment centre right away," was her advice. I remember at the time thinking, "I must be an alcoholic if she says so," and that treatment would be like a holiday: 28 days in Napa Valley at a hospital treatment centre (now there's irony for you—a treatment centre in the wine capital of the US). I thought, "I have nothing to lose, it will get me away from my (ex) husband long enough to gain some perspective." So I decided on Sunday, after talking to her on Saturday, and was on the plane Monday morning.

That I went into a 28-day program in an addiction treatment centre outside of San Francisco was the best thing that could have happened. Looking back on it, I believe it saved my life.

I remember being terrified as the security guard picked me up at the airport, and as we drove up Sanatorium Road I thought, "What have I gotten myself into?"

For 28 days I ate healthy, vegetarian food, attended counseling sessions, learned about family dynamics and the role I had taken on as the oldest child, and I learned to cry and let down my guard. I attended AA meetings and practiced saying "Hi I'm Tana and I'm an alcoholic." I began to get perspective about what was real and what was created by others and how I wasn't responsible for all the world's problems, as I'd once thought I was.

After three weeks the counselor at the centre asked me why I was there. I said, "I must be in denial." And he said, "If you're in denial, you don't say you're in denial…" He said I could stay in the program if I wanted to, but that they didn't see alcoholism as an issue for me—except that I was close to crossing the line and might want to watch my step and be more aware for the future.

So I stayed for the final week and "graduation." I continued to work-out twice a day, learn more about how to deal with stress, what AA programs were all about, and other amazingly important things.

Before I left I had to set up an aftercare program for when I was at home. The after-care program got me into counseling for about a year. That was when I started sorting through my personality and seeing how I was living my life in survival mode—making destructive choices because I hated myself—rather than reaching for my potential.

I had no idea what my potential was, just that something wasn't working for me.

After I returned from the treatment centre and a few years of a low-key life, I owned a clothing store (in the early 1990's). I believed that getting to go on shopping sprees (buy shows) for the store and having all the clothes I wanted would make me happy. So I created the store, and realized that there was still something missing. I had no sense of who I was and of my value as a person just because I am a human being on this earth.

During my first marriage I lost myself completely.

After my marriage broke down, my lifestyle was still destructive as I continued to search for an external source of internal peace and self esteem.

Later in my life when I had achieved my MBA and was moving up in the corporate world, I began to question what it all meant. I had the material success that I was "supposed to want" by our cultural standards—so I could take more cabs, eat at better restaurants and take more holidays. But success had lost its meaning. I knew there was something more.

I began working with a Jungian analyst and focused on dream therapy. This was helpful to see the layers of old "stuff" that was limiting me, to work through them, and allow them to loosen their hold on my life.

In 2000 when I moved to Chicago and consulted in the US, I again sought out support as, I believe, I was burned out when I moved there and really went on the journey for my ego.

The stress was beginning to show physically and at its worst I had cold sores on a weekly basis. I wanted to know that I was smart enough and capable enough to "play in that big US game." Having an MBA and making the big money in the US was what I thought I was supposed to aspire to, and achieve.

I thought that if clients sought me out and wanted to work with me, and if others saw me as smart, then I must be a good person and have value.

Progress, apparently, isn't linear.... Here I was back at the question of "worth" as a human being, again.

I realized that my life was back in Canada and that I needed to get off the ladder I was climbing to who knows where.... I also realized at some point in time that I was happier in my life when I was choosing it—when I was creating it and not waiting for someone or something to make me feel better or to rescue me.

When I moved back to Vancouver and achieved my dream job—to be on the executive team of a multi-billion dollar company, I again burnt out and this time it manifested physically for six months as adrenal fatigue, hormonal imbalance and vertigo. I knew something was still blocked and I sought support from my doctor, a naturopath, and a counselor.

At the same time I was blessed with the opportunity to attend the New Ventures West professional coaching course[87] where a big part of the year-long program was developing my capacity as a person so I could be present for my clients.

Between the counseling and the coaching program, as well as the nutritional and philosophical support of my doctor (who has an approach that includes alternative practices) and the naturopath, I learned to come back to balance again and again and to integrate it into my life. I also learned to live with inner clarity awareness of Authentic Self versus personality/ego, and to live with compassion and joy versus fear and anger, more of the time.

A huge shift came from an introduction to the Enneagram system and learning that I was a type three or "achiever"—big surprise! The real learning, though, was the new awareness that I was getting my self-esteem from external sources, and not from my inner clarity. I needed to be a successful _____(fill in the blank) and an executive to get my self-esteem. Failure was too distressing to even contemplate. I suddenly woke up for the first time to the fact that I was still living my life in a way that wasn't honoring my Authentic Self or my potential.

At the time of writing it is 2013. For the past eight years I have been introduced to a strong foundation of practices that support me in living from what my heart wants, and leading from authenticity, more of the time. This is in contrast to living only as part of my potential, as my personality or who I am when living from my automatic or default way of being. While my personality has helped me be very successful, parts of it no longer serve me.

Some of the personal work I've done so far on my inner development, includes learning how to do the following:

---

87   http://www.newventureswest.com/

- Be aware of my intrinsic value as a human simply by virtue of my "being" on the earth—as a physical manifestation of the universe or god or however you choose to think about it
- Accept life, practice awareness, and let go of image
- Feel and articulate emotions as they arise and then dissipate
- Manage my inner critic
- Breathe through the "arc of intense energy" that occurs during stress and stay present in situations of increasingly intense energy
- Have difficult conversations in which I feel intimidated
- Manage conflict and clear small annoyances before they become big issues
- Listen to my intuition as I learn to integrate the three centres of intelligence (head: thinking mind; heart: emotions; body: sensing and intuition)
- Accept and be curious about anxiousness that occurs before the next layer of personality unfolds
- Accept and integrate my shadow aspects of personality
- Become aware of and let go of the unhelpful aspects of my Personality/ego
- Become aware of and constantly let go of my (many) addictions including an addiction to the adrenaline hits of "getting things done," to being recognized for my work, to good red wine, to chai tea, to "doing," to using caffeine to "not" feel the discomfort of being tired
- Forgive myself and others for being only human
- Live with compassion more of the time
- Manifest the positive and pay attention to how it increases my vibration level
- Live congruent with the Law of Attraction (the science of getting more of what you want and less of what you don't want) to support me on my journey (through acting daily in ways that are congruent with my Authentic Self)
- Ground my (at times) delusional optimism in reality, to support better decision making
- Let go of control, and trust that what is needed will show up as it's meant to
- Notice my resistance to day-to-day life, and let go in order to either accept it or, at times, even embrace life with enthusiasm
- Accept support and love freely

- Let go of attachment and constantly comparing, and appreciate how freeing this can be
- Learn what "enough" is and how little we really need for sustenance
- Articulate my philosophy and approach to nutrition and wellness, and notice how the medical model, alternative approaches, and faith can all play a part
- Be humbled and re-centre over and over to strengthen my relationships
- Be in business in a way that is heart-centred, co-creative, and invites abundance
- Live with energy levels at a natural, non-caffeinated pace, and
- Stay present through trauma and, by actually feeling emotions, support others to feel theirs as well.

Each day this list grows as authenticity unfolds.

The possibilities for my life are endless now, and the pace is manageable (most of the time—I do still find the active practice of balance a challenge at times). I have more inner peace and self-confidence than I've ever had, I am "awake" more of the time to my old patterns and potential blocks, and I constantly work on and adjust my thoughts and behaviours to be more in line with my Authentic Self.

I am clear that I am valuable simply because I'm on this Earth—not because I'm a successful something, or because others like me.

It's a very different way of being.

There are be times in my life when I need a guide and times when I am okay on my own. When I get stuck, or when I plateau and want to move forward, or when there is something holding me back, then I find a guide (or a guide finds me). Inner development has for 25 years been such an essential investment in my success as a leader and an individual. I hope to keep this philosophy always.

It has been an incredible journey to this point and I am grateful for it all. I am also learning to be more comfortable in the "not knowing" about the future. I am, after all, manifesting it in each moment as I live authentically, more of the time.

Authenticity

Grounded
Heart-centered
Able to see ego in the moment
for what it is...

Old, automatic patterns
Unconsciously on autopilot
Once awakened
are seen for what they are...

Merely thoughts
passing like clouds...

When I stay present and live in the moment
Choosing the vertical life
connected to source
intelligence moves through me
the answers come...

Clarity in the moment...

Authenticity.

- Tana Heminsley

BIBLIOGRAPHY

The following is a bibliography of the books and other resources that contributed to this Authentic Leadership philosophy and work.

Bosman, Manie. "What is the single most important quality of an effective leader?" *Linked In Survey* (Link lost), Feb 22, 2012.

Caldwell, Christine. *Getting our Bodies Back—Recovery, Healing, and Transformation through Body-Centered Psychotherapy.* Boston: Shambhala Publications, Inc., 1996.

Carlson, Richard, and Joseph Bailey. *Slowing down to the Speed of Life— How to create a more peaceful, simpler life from the inside out.* New York: HarperCollins Books, 1997.

Chade-Meng, Tan. *Everyday Compassion at Google.* TED Talks Video, http://www.youtube.com/watch?v=yTR4sAD_4qM, posted April 2011. http://www.ted.com/talks/lang/eng/chade_meng_tan_every-day_compassion_at_google.html

Cherry, Kendra. *What is Cognitive Dissonance?* http://psychology.about.com/od/cognitivepsychology/f/dissonance.htm , 2012.

Chodron, Pema. *Start Where you Are—A Guide to Compassionate Living.* Boston, Mass: Shambhala Classics, 1994.

Collins, Jim. *Good to Great—Why Some Companies Make the Leap... and Others Don't.* New York: HarperCollins Publishers, 2001.

Covey, Stephen. *Seven Habits of Highly Effective People.* https://www.stephencovey.com/7habits/7habits-habit5.php

"Driving Employee Performance and Retention Through Engagement - A Qualitative Analysis of the effectiveness of Employee Engagement Strategies." *Corporate Leadership Council*, Corporate Executive Board, 2004.

Effects of Stress, http://www.webmd.com/balance/stress-management/stress-management-effects-of-stress

Ferarri, Bernard T. The Executive's Guide to Better Listening, *McKinsey Quarterly*, Feb, 2012. http://www.mckinseyquarterly.com/Governance/Leadership/The_executives_guide_to_better_listening_2931

George, Bill. *True North – Discover your Authentic Leadership.* San Francisco: Josey Bass, 2007.

George, Bill, and Peter Sims, Andrew N. McLean, and Diana Mayer. "Discovering Your Authentic Leadership." *Harvard Business Review*, Volume 85: No 2 (February 2007), 129 - 138.

Goleman, Daniel. *Primal Leadership—Learning to Lead with Emotional Intelligence.* Boston: Harvard Business School Press, 2002.

Goleman, Daniel. "What Makes a Leader?", *Harvard Business Review*, http://hbr.org/2004/01/what-makes-a-leader/ar/1, 1998.

Hawkins, David R. M.D., Ph.D.. *Power vs Force, The Hidden Determinants of Human Behaviour.* 3rd ed. Carlsbad, CA: Hay House, Inc. (Originally published in Sedona, Ariz.: Veritas Publishing), 2002.

Kornfield, Jack. *A Path With Heart – A Guide through the Perils and Promises of Spiritual Life.* New York: Bantam Books, 1993.

O Dream Boards, http://www.oprah.com/packages/o-dream-board.html, 2012.

Our Deepest Fear, poem by Marianne Williamson

Paint Cans, Poem reproduced with permission from Claire McInnes

Pink, Daniel. *DRiVE—the Surprising Truth About What Motivates Us.* New York: River Head Books; The Penguin Group, 2009.

Professional Coaching Course, New Ventures West, http://www.newventureswest.com.

Riso, Don Richard, and Russ Hudson. *The Wisdom of the Enneagram: The Complete Guide to Psychological and Spiritual Growth for the Nine Personality Types.* New York: A Bantham Book, 1999.

Sinetar, Marsha. *Do What you Love, the Money will Follow.* New York: Dell Publishing, 1987.

Sutherland, Kate. *Make Light Work—10 Tools for Inner Knowing.* Vancouver, BC: Insight Press, 2010.

Taylor, Katy. "Ego and Essence." *The Enneagram Monthly*, November 2008, Issue 153, http://www.enneagraminstitute.com/articles/NArtEgoAndEssence.asp

The Evolutionary Layers of the Human Brain, http://thebrain.mcgill.ca/flash/d/d_05/d_05_cr/d_05_cr_her/d_05_cr_her.html, 2012.

BIBLIOGRAPHY

The Guest House, poem by Rumi as shared by my teacher Sarita Chawla, Professional Coach Course, New Ventures West, 2005.

Tolle, Eckhart. *A New Earth—Awaken to your Life's Purpose*. New York: Penguin Group, 2005.

Tolle, Eckhart. *A New Earth—Awakening to Your Life's Purpose - 52 Inspirational Cards*. New World Library Namaste Publishing.

Values (List of words), http://www.gurusoftware.com/GuruNet/Personal/Topics/Values.htm

Values (Definition) http://www.orednet.org/~jflory/205/205_val_intro.htm

Wheatley, Margaret J.. *Leadership and the New Science—Discovering Order in a Chaotic World*. San Francisco: Berrett-Koehler Publishers, 1999.

Wilson, Dr. James, N.D., D.C., Ph.D.. *Adrenal Fatigue – The 21st Century Stress Syndrome*. 13th printing. Petaluma, CA: Smart Publications, 2009.

Wisdom 2.0 Conference http://wisdom2summit.com/

Wise, Anna. *The High-Performance Mind – Mastering Brainwaves for Insight, Healing, and Creativity*. 2nd ed. New York: Tarcher/Penguin, 1995.

APPENDIX A
ACTION WORKSHEETS

Use the following action worksheets to complete each step of the Authentic You™ Personal Planning System. Once you have completed each step, transfer the final product either into your Personal Learning Journal, or onto your Authentic You™ Poster.

1. Remember your Authentic Self (page 168)
2. Articulate your values (page 178)
3. Discover your purpose (page 185)
4. Clarify your leadership principles (page 191)
5. Create your life vision (page 196)
6. Assess your work-life balance (page 199)
7. Reflect on your awakening and the implications for your leadership (page 206)
8. Set your goals (page 209)
9. Create your inner development plan (page 214)
10. Putting it into practice (page 227)

ACTION WORKSHEET - STEP #1
REMEMBER YOUR AUTHENTIC SELF

Use one or all of the following exercises to support you to remember your Authentic Self.

There is an important distinction between authentic leaders and other leaders: Authentic leaders understand that their potential is broader than what they are aware of at this moment.

Their current awareness may include aspects of themselves that have developed to this point in their lives. They may be aware of their strengths and they may also be aware of their opportunities to be more effective. They may have noticed their tendency to react too quickly, or to interpret situations incorrectly, and the impact this has had on themselves and others.

They may also be unaware of other aspects of self that are undiscovered or more accurately have been forgotten—joy, compassion, creativity as well as the ability to be clear and firm; aspects that are covered up by the layers of personality.

The distinction between parts of ourselves that we are familiar with and that may act as strengths or obstacles, and our deeper, clearer, selves that we may have covered up is referred to as personality (or ego) and Authentic Self.

Authentic Self is who you are when at your best—a creative and compassionate person with the unique qualities that make you who you are. It is your potential and your birthright.

Personality includes the aspects of self that develop from birth to adulthood as a result of influences and experiences in our lives—those that are helpful (strengths) and those that are no longer helpful (self-limiting thoughts and beliefs).

Beneath the layers of personality lives the true nature of the person— the Authentic Self —always there and waiting to be rediscovered and remembered. The number of layers of personality, particularly those that are unhelpful or unhealthy, depends on many factors including genetics, upbringing, culture and lifestyle.

Generally, we do not experience our Essence and its many aspects because our awareness is so dominated by our personality. But as we learn to bring awareness to our personality, it becomes more transparent, and we are able to experience our essence more directly.[88]

Your Authentic Self shines through more often as you understand and engage your strengths, see the self-limiting thoughts and behaviours for what they are, and let them go in order to make choices aligned with who you truly are.

This first exercise is an important first step, orienting your thinking to your potential for who you are when at your best.

Before beginning, center, relax and be open to the exercise you are about to complete.

1. Personal Research

a) Reflect on the following questions for yourself. Then ask 3 or 4 people—your family, colleagues, friends, boss and/or team—to write down their perception of you. Ask them:

- Who am I when at my best?
- What are a few words you would use to describe me when I am at my best?
- What is my gift in the world? What am I good at? What do you think I should be doing in my next chapter?

b) Write down your own reflection about yourself here. Words that describe you when at your best are:

1.

2.

3.

4.

5.

---

88   Ibid.

c) Write their names and responses below:

Respondent One – Name and Responses:

Respondent Two – Name and Responses:

Respondent Three – Name and Responses:

Complete one or all of the following exercises before completing your final list.

2. Self-reflection—Life steps / Career / Life Journey / Educational Training

Complete the following table for each job or career step you have taken to your life at this point. Include your age, the job you had at that time or the name of the position you held, whether the experience was fulfilling (+) or not (-) and 1-2 words that describe your way of being when you were most fulfilled. The first few lines provide an example:

Your age or the year (approx.):	Life steps / Job or Position / Educational Training:	Level of fulfillment you experienced during this time. Show visually with one or more of each (+) or (-):	Words to describe your way of being when you were most fulfilled:
18	Finished high school	-	
25	Writer for local newspaper	+++	Courageous Curious Empathetic
33	Got divorced	---------	Resentful Vengeful Sad Resigned

3. Complete a 360 Review

a) Complete a 360 Review with your supervisor, peers, people who report to you, friends or family. There are many different types and forms of 360 review.

Use the following questions to create your own simple questionnaire and feel free to adapt it in a way that feels right for you:

- What are my strengths?
- What are my opportunities for development?
- What two things do I not know about myself that would be helpful for me to know (may be blind spots for me): Positive and Negative.
- What beliefs do I have that support me to be effective?
- What beliefs do I have that may be getting in my way?
- Any other feedback for me?

b) Write the words that stand out from the responses that describe you at your best, below:

Respondent One and words they used to describe me:

Respondent Two and words they used to describe me:

Respondent Three and words they used to describe me:

Respondent Four and words they used to describe me:

4. Use a Personality or other Self-Assessment to understand your potential

Assessments can be helpful when completing your personal research. These can include the Riso-Hudson Enneagram Type Indicator, Myers Briggs Type Indicator Assessment (MBTI) ®, Insight Inventory ®, Strengthsfinder Assessment, TTI Emotional Quotient Assessment, Authentic Leadership 360 Assessment, etc. There are many more available. They can also be helpful to refer to again and again over time to develop new awareness.

a) Complete one or more personality or other self-assessments to understand your potential. Write the words that stand out in your assessment results that describe you when at your best, here:

Assessment:
Words this Assessment provided me to describe my Authentic Self:

Assessment:
Words this Assessment provided me to describe my Authentic Self:

Assessment:
Words this Assessment provided me to describe my Authentic Self:

5. Exercise and Reflection: Using the Enneagram to discover your potential

Use *The Wisdom of the Enneagram* book together with this exercise to discover your potential as Authentic Self.

A) DISCOVER YOUR PREFERRED TYPE

First, take one of the many free online tests available, or the complete RHETI test (approximately $10 USD) using the link to the Enneagram resources on the homepage at http://www.enneagraminstitute.com/Tests_Battery.asp and/or complete the test in *The Wisdom of the Enneagram* book called the QUEST (Quick Enneagram Sorting Test)[89].

Using your results, notice the Enneagram type that has the highest score (e.g. Type Three—The Achiever)—if you are here, you may have discovered your type.

If there is more than one type with a high score (e.g. you score seventeen points on each of types Three, Seven, and Eight) on your results, do the following for each:

- Using *The Wisdom of the Enneagram* book, turn to the chapter that is focused on each type. There are 15 questions for each that will help you to discern which one fits you.
- Answer the questions for each of the types and score them. The type with the highest score is the one to work with.
- If there are still several with close scores, use your life and career journey forms and your Authentic You™ Personal Learning Journal to reflect on and identify the core issue for your type. This is identified and described at the beginning of each of the chapters for the nine types.

B) REVIEW INFORMATION ABOUT YOUR TYPE AND GLIMPSE YOUR POTENTIAL

A note regarding your inner critic when working with the Enneagram, or any other assessment: The inner critic will want to focus immediately on the challenges and things that are "wrong" with this type. It will become judgmental and can shut down your learning if you focus immediately on these aspects. While they are helpful to be aware of, we intentionally focus first on your potential, in order to anchor your experience and awareness there.

---

89   Wisdom of the Enneagram, Ibid, page 13—15.

Read the following short sections:
- Description of the type—first 1—2 pages of the chapter (stop at "Childhood Pattern)
- Potential for this type of person when they are most developed— read descriptions for Level 1—3 (Healthy)
- "Building on the (type)'s strengths" or "The (type's) Gifts"
- "The Emergence of Essence"—last page of the chapter

6. Describe your Authentic Self
Reflect on all of the responses you have gathered and the research you have completed, including your own thoughts and reflections, and compile a list of words that describe you when at your best.

Write your final list here:

Authentic Me—I am:

1.

2.

3.

4.

5.

6.

7.

8.

9.

10.

7. Review and Reflect

Read the list to yourself, aloud, while looking in the mirror (or to a friend) beginning with "I am....".

Notice how it feels and what your body language and tone are like as you do. Write down what your experience was like using the following space:

How I felt:

What I noticed about my body language and tone:

What emotions arose during this exercise, if any:

What this experience was like for me:

What I am learning about myself as a result:

Once you complete the exercises and articulate the words to describe your Authentic Self, make adjustments and transfer these into your Authentic You™ Personal Learning Journal or on to your Authentic You™ Poster. If the latter, be sure to have a second sheet so one can be for a draft copy. This will help to allay any judgments your inner critic may have about it needing to be perfect to put it on the written page.

ACTION WORKSHEET – STEP #2
ARTICULATE YOUR VALUES

Use the following action worksheet to articulate your values.

Values are deeply held beliefs about what is important to you for your life. They are words that describe what is important to you.

"They are believed to be what people care about deeply and serve as standards for judging acts, guiding behavior, evaluating social conditions, and give meaning to life.

Values are thought to be relatively stable, much longer lasting and less subject to change than opinions so that they are not subject to sudden shifts or impulses of the moment." [90]

Finally, they can be prioritized to give emphasis to different values at different times in your life.

1. Prepare for this exercise

Before beginning, center, relax and open to the exercises you are about to complete.

Review your description of authentic self from Step #1, reflecting on your potential and how it feels to understand who you are at your best.

2. Reflect on past situations and trade offs

There may have been times in your leadership career and your life when you needed to stop and consider what steps were appropriate to take next. These could have ranged from making a decision about a new career opportunity, to whether to go to university, to whether to have a family.

There are situations each day where you need to make decisions, and values—whether you know them overtly, or consider them intuitively—are providing the guideposts.

Write down two situations in which you had to take time to reflect on a decision based on your deeply held conviction about the right thing to do.

---

90   Source: Values, http://www.orednet.org/~jflory/205/205_val_intro.htm

For example—whether or not to take a promotion in which there would be much more time at work and travel required that would take you away from your family for the equivalent of 5 months a year.

   a)

   b)

   c) Write down words that describe what you believe in, that leads you to the criteria for making these decisions. For example—Importance of family; love of travel; love of my work; stimulation of adventure. Write your words here:

3. Review a list of values words

After reflecting on what values are, and some situations in your life that have required trade-offs based on what is deeply important to you, it is time to choose the words that describe your values.

COMMON PERSONAL VALUES WORDS[91]

Accomplishment, Success	Flair	Progress
Accountability	Freedom	Prosperity, Wealth
Accuracy	Friendship	Punctuality
Adventure	Fun	Quality of work
All for one & one for all	Global view	Regularity Resourcefulness
Beauty	Good will	Respect for others
Calm, quietude, peace	Goodness	Responsiveness
Challenge	Gratitude	Results-oriented
Change	Hard work	Rule of Law
Cleanliness, orderliness	Harmony	Safety
Collaboration	Honesty	Satisfying others
Commitment	Honor	Security
Communication	Independence	Self-givingness
Community	Inner peace, calm, quietude	Self-reliance
Competence	Innovation	Service
Competition	Integrity	(to others, society)
Concern for others	Justice	Simplicity
Content over form	Knowledge	Skill
Continuous improvement	Leadership	Speed
Cooperation	Love, Romance	Spirit in life (using)
Coordination	Loyalty	Stability
Country, love of (patriotism)	Maximum utilization	Standardization

---

91   Source: Values, http://www.gurusoftware.com/GuruNet/Personal/Topics/Values.htm
For a list of Business values see: http://www.gurusoftware.com/GuruNet/Business/Values.
htm

Creativity	(of time, resources)	Status
Customer satisfaction	Meaning	Strength
Decisiveness	Merit	Succeed; A will to-
Delight of being, joy	Money	Success, Achievement
Democracy	Openness	Systemization
Discipline	Peace, Non-violence	Teamwork
Discovery	Perfection (e.g. of details)	Timeliness
Ease of Use	Personal Growth	Tolerance
Efficiency	Pleasure	Tradition
Equality	Positive attitude	Tranquility
Excellence	Power	Trust
Fairness	Practicality	Truth
Faith	Preservation	Unity
Family	Privacy	Variety
Family feeling	Problem Solving	Wisdom

Referring to the list, select and write down words that describe your values:

1.

2.

3.

4.

5.

6.

7.

4. Test out your values

Think of three situations at work and in your personal life in which you need to make an important decision. Write them here. For example, *I am returning to work after maternity leave and I want to be both effective as a leader as well as with my family, and maintain my wellness*; or *I need to decide on a new product offering at work that may have potential negative impacts on a business partner I am working with*).

Situation One:

Situation Two:

Situation Three:

Next, for each of the situations, reflect on your values and what guidance they provide you. List them in order of importance to get even clearer about the emphasis you want to place on different parts of your life. Complete the following:

As I reflect on each of the above situations, my values provide the following guidance (example):

- Values (in order of importance: family, wellness, career, education, spirituality, fun

- Situation: (Mary is returning to work after maternity leave) Mary's value of family (first priority) means that she may only want to work four days a week; her value for wellness means that she will make time for rest by booking time at the gym 3x/week for "me" time; and her value of education will have to drop in priority as she forgoes the MBA she has been thinking of doing, for the foreseeable future.

Complete your assessment using the blank table here:

My values in order of importance:	
Situation One:	
Situation Two:	
Situation Three:	

5. Review and Reflect

Read the list to yourself, aloud, while looking in the mirror (or to a friend) beginning with "I value ….".

Notice how it feels and what arises for you in terms of emotions or thoughts, as you do. Write down what your experience was like using the following space:

How I felt:

What I noticed about my thoughts:

What emotions arose during this exercise, if any:

What this experience was like for me:

What I am learning about myself as a result:

Remember, this is just a starting point and your values may evolve.

They may also change in importance at different times in your life. For example, one person values travel and working hard. Then they have children they have a new value of time with family. Their focus has changed and family time "trumps" travel for the first few years of raising their children; or they may incorporate travel in a new way into their lives—instead of travelling internationally, they may choose to travel close to home, or in a way that the children can participate.

For another great exercise to clarify and rank your values, see http://mikedesjardins.com/tag/core-values/.

ACTION WORKSHEET – STEP #3
DISCOVER YOUR PURPOSE

Use the following action worksheet to articulate your purpose. Authentic leaders are clear about what their higher purpose is, or what they were intended for in their life.

Your purpose is the reason beyond yourself that provides meaning for your life. It is how you are meant to leave your mark in the world—how you are meant to contribute, and your legacy for your family.

In order to become clear about your purpose, there are several things you can do:

1. Prepare for this exercise
Begin by relaxing, centering and opening to the exercises you are about to complete.

2. Review your research from Steps One and Two
Review your material from Step #1: Articulating Authentic Self: the life review, the information from friends, family, and co-workers, as well as the results of your personality assessments. In addition, review your values. Reflect on how it feels to understand who you are at your best and what is important to you.

Then, complete the following statements:

My strengths are (what I'm good at and what I love)....

When I do the following activities, I notice that my energy builds....

I love contributing by doing the following....

My passion in life is....

My higher purpose is....

If you are unclear, review and complete the following:

3. Conduct interviews

Conduct informal interviews with at least three people who are living their lives and contributing in ways that you are curious about or interested in (For example, you know a person who has started a business in ecotourism and you have always been curious about it—especially as the person was formerly a doctor and in her/his late 40's is when the life change took place; another person is a lawyer and you think you might like to be a lawyer and represent people when they have been in an accidents; another person has written a book about time management and effective organizing; another makes jewelry for a living.)

Ask them to have or tea/coffee with you or set up a call or face-to-face meeting. Ask if they will be willing to share their story and insights with you. For each person, ask them the following questions and record your responses here:

Question:	Interviewee Responses:
Can you describe what it is that you do?	
How is what you do meaningful to you?	
How did you get to where you are? What has been your journey?	
What made you make the changes to your life?	
What things would I need to consider if I were to do something similar?	
What are the challenges with what you do?	
What do you love about living this way?	
What does a typical day in your life look like?	
What does the typical month look like?	

After you have conducted the interviews, ask yourself the following questions, and record your responses here:

What I notice:	Interviewee Responses:
Does thinking about this as a possibility excite me for my life?	
Is there other information I need to gather about their occupation?	
Does my energy build or diminish when I hear about the way this person is living?	

4. Shift or let go of self-limiting beliefs

You may have a difficult time seeing new possibilities for your leadership and your life if you can only imagine one way forward—the way it has always been, or if you notice that you have lots of reasons why something different is just not possible.

Review the chapter on inner development, as well as the action worksheet for creating your inner development plan. You may need to spend several months working on shifting beliefs before you see different possibilities for what you are intended for or what your purpose is.

If you are not sure how to proceed, your inner development plan may include one thing—find a trusted person to get support from for a targeted period of time.

5. Create your Purpose

Remind your inner critic that this is just a draft, and so you can let go of the pressure it will want to put on you. Combine what you have written above into a list and write it here.

My purpose in the world is to do the following:

Point one:

Point two:

Point three:

Next, combine these points into one statement—My purpose in the world is to do the following:

6. Review and reflect

Read the statement to yourself aloud, while looking in the mirror (or to a friend) beginning with "My purpose is ….".

Notice how it feels and what arises for you in terms of emotions or thoughts, as you do. Write down what your experience was like using the following space:

How I felt:

What I noticed about my thoughts:

What emotions arose during this exercise, if any:

What this experience was like for me:

What I am learning about myself as a result:

Leave the statement for a few days and adjust it until it feels aligned with who you are. When it represents who you are, you will experience a sense of calm and deep knowing—a feeling of coming home.

ACTION WORKSHEET – STEP #4
CLARIFY YOUR LEADERSHIP PRINCIPLES

Use the following action worksheet to articulate your leadership principles:

EXERCISE

1. Prepare Personally
Begin by relaxing, centering and opening to these exercises.

2. Complete a self-reflection
Reflect on your what you've learned about your Authentic Self, values and purpose.

3. Answer these questions
Answer the following questions and write your responses below.

When I am being my Authentic Self, without the limiting voices of my ego, the "shoulds", or my inner critic, what is it that I love to do at work or in my business?

What do I love to do that will support creating a great environment where people I work with can feel comfortable to be authentic as well?

How will I contribute to making the world a better place through my business practices?

How will these business practices contribute to abundance for myself, the business, and the world?

4. Create a list of Leadership Principles

Once you have reflected on these questions, create a list of words or statements that are your leadership principles—how your Authentic Self, your values, vision for your life translates into your day-to-day activities.

These principles are transferable across industries or organizations, as well as in your personal life, and they provide a way to bring forth your Authentic Self, more of the time.

For example:

Purpose	Value	Leadership Principle
Supporting people to be the best they can be	Authenticity	Talk about the importance of authenticity when having conversations and model it in your leadership—both 1:1 and in groups; with peers, direct reports and supervisors; with customers.
Supporting people to be the best they can be	Sustainability	Create the conditions for a low-to-no carbon footprint; model it in your own behaviours for your team and in your personal life

Supporting people to be the best they can be	Connection	Facilitate team-building workshops in which people can develop community as they learn about their potential as a person

Again, these are transferable principles that you can take to any job or volunteer position, at any time.

My leadership principles are:

My values are:	My leadership principles are:

6. Use your Leadership Principles each day

Using the list of leadership principles you created, plan to incorporate them into your day-to-day activities by completing the following:

List the current activities I do in my job:

Review the list and reflect on the following:

What percentage of the activities that I do each day are aligned with my principles?

What can I do differently to bring a higher percentage of my day-to-day leadership activities into alignment with my leadership principles?

Are there activities that do not align, that I can given away to someone else who likes to do them? Who else could do the activities for me?

Is there any support I would need to have in order to implement my leadership principles?

7. Review and reflect

Read the statement to yourself aloud, while looking in the mirror (or to a friend) beginning with "My leadership principles are ....".

As you read it, notice how it feels and what arises for you in terms of emotions or thoughts. Write down what your experience was like using the following space:

How I felt:

What I noticed about my thoughts:

What emotions arose during this exercise, if any:

What this experience was like for me:

What I am learning about myself as a result:

ACTION WORKSHEET – STEP #5
CREATE YOUR LIFE VISION

Use the following action worksheet to articulate your vision for your life.

1. Prepare Personally
Begin by relaxing, centering and opening to these exercises.

2. Reflect on what you have learned
Reflect on your what you've learned about your Authentic Self, values and purpose and leadership principles.

3. Gather your materials and Create your Life-Vision Board
Complete the following steps to create your life-vision board:

a) Gather 5—6 magazines that represent who you are at this point in your life, family photos that are meaningful, and other materials that you might want to incorporate into a collage. Purchase a poster board (in a colour that speaks to you) and gather together a pair of scissors, some scotch tape, and some coloured pens.

Put on your most comfortable clothing, find a space that feels energizing for you to create in, and put on your favourite music. Give yourself up to 2 hours (or whatever is needed) to create your life-vision board.

Note: While this is a lovely exercise to do with your partner or significant other, it can be helpful to leave that for later. For now, the focus is creating your vision.

(optional) Complete the following short visualization exercise.

b) Close your eyes and either sit in a comfortable chair, or lie down on the floor on a yoga mat, or on a sofa. Spend 10—30 minutes thinking of a perfect day in your life in the future. Ask yourself the following:

What does it look like?
What do you experience?

What does it feel like?

What are all the activities that are occurring at this moment in your life vision?

How does it include your personal life? Your Work-life?

After your visualization exercise, bring your awareness back into the room and begin your creation.

c) Flip through the magazines and other materials you have gathered, paying attention to images and words that call to you. This is a right-brain exercise so remind yourself to let go of analyzing for the moment as you enjoy creating. Cut the images and words out and set aside.

d) Once you have gathered all the images and words that feel right at this time, begin to assemble them on the poster board and tape them in place as a collage. After you have completed your life-vision board, write your name and the date in one corner or the board so you remember when you created it.

In the future, as you make more life-vision boards, you will be able to follow how they change over time.

3. Review and Reflect

Review the story of your life-vision board aloud to yourself (or to a friend or significant other) beginning with "My life vision is ....".

Notice how it feels and what arises for you in terms of emotions or thoughts, as you do. Write down what your experience was like using the following space:

How I felt:

What I noticed about my thoughts:

What emotions arose during this exercise, if any:

What this experience was like for me:

What I am learning about myself as a result:

Notice how it feels to practice being vulnerable and sharing something deeply important to you with another person.

Review your life-vision board on a regular basis (some spend time with it each day) and then put it away. By reminding yourself about it and leaving it on the back burner so it can "percolate" and bubble away, you are allowing the next steps on your path to emerge.

Once you have achieved a major milestone in your life (this may be years later), review the life-vision board again and see how your actions relate to the vision you created.

It is common for people to share with others that they are amazed that something that they put on their life-vision board, and then completely forgot about, has come to fruition in their life.

ACTION WORKSHEET – STEP #6
ASSESS YOUR WORK-LIFE BALANCE

Use the following action worksheet to assess your current vs. optimal work-life balance.

1. Prepare Personally
Begin by relaxing, centering and opening to these exercises.

2. Reflect on what you have learned
Reflect on what you've learned about your Authentic Self, values, purpose, leadership principles and life vision. This provides the context for understanding the awakening that may be occurring, as well as assessing your current vs. optimal work-life balance.

3. Complete your Work-life Balance Assessment
Refer to the following diagram and complete the exercise below.

Work-life balance assessment—example of one person's current level of work-life balance:

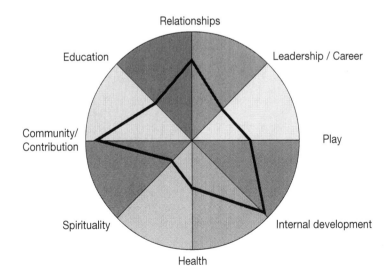

This diagram shows, in a simple way, the different areas of this person's life and the amount of effort/energy they are spending in each of them. The outside of the circle is the optimal level and the point on each line for each piece of the "pie" of your life shows the current level for each area.

The diagram gives an indication about how this leader may be feeling out of balance and where may want to make adjustments. For example, this person is happy with the level of energy/time spent on community and contribution, relationships, and internal development. One area to focus on for improvement is health and spirituality.

Instructions for completing your work-life balance assessment

Step one, identify and name the different parts of your life—relationships, career, contribution, abundance—use your own words/labels for what is meaningful for you.

Step two, assume the outer edge of the circle is your optimal amount of that component in your life (i.e. you want to have some education in your life through continuing education at your community college, but you don't want to pursue a PhD). Assume the centre of the circle is a 0 and the outer edge is a 10. This provides a simple way of showing the relative importance of each component to you.

Step three, draw a line from the centre of the circle to the outer edge, for each part of your life. Place a dot on the line for each component to show where you are currently. For example in the diagram above, it shows community / contribution as about an 8 out of 10. This means that the person currently has quite a lot of this relative to, say, health. When they assess their whole life, they may want to make adjustments to focus more on health. Or maybe not. The system is designed to be flexible and to fit each person's life and language—there are no judgments attached (that one is better than another)— this is merely the current state.

Step four, once you have a dot on each line, join them with a line to show the relative "balance" in your life currently.

Step five, reflect on what this tells you as you become more self-aware. Think about what lifestyle adjustments you might want to make, if any, to shift the balance to one that is optimal for you at this time.

MY CURRENT LIFE BALANCE:

4. Choose what to improve

Decide on two or three parts of your life you'd like to adjust in order to have more balance. Write your response here.

Given my values and my current balance, some areas of my life where I would like to adjust my balance would be _____, _____, and _____. (i.e. career, health and play)

5. Decide on the level of improvement

Consider the following questions and write down your responses, as you reflect on what will be needed in order to make adjustments.

What are the realities (family and business) and needs to consider and respect when looking at possibilities for trade-offs?

Do I know all the possible solutions? If not, who could support me to think through them? (i.e. we have a large project coming up for which I'll have to work weekends for the next 2 months—I'll need to check with my peers/boss in case this may go longer).

What will be the trade-offs if I make adjustments and how can my values help me decide the right way to make the adjustment? (i.e. for the next 2 months I may need to ask my parents to support my partner and I by taking our child for 1 day a weekend; I'll book a long weekend away with my family once the project is over).

What challenges or obstacles might arise while making changes to have more balance? (i.e. I may not be used to asking my boss for the day off needed for the long weekend I want to book; I may not be used to asking my parents—or friends—for help.)

6. Decide Who will support you

What support might I need? Whom could I ask to support me?

7. Create a sImple plan

My simple plan for beginning to practice balance in my life (keep it simple so it's more realistic):

Belief I will need to shift and Benefit:
Belief I'll need to shift
More time for me to rest (as work consists of back-to-back meetings and we have 2 kids).
Benefit—I'll be more effective as a boss and a parent as I'll have more perspective and feel less resentful.

How I will reframe this belief:
That time to care for myself is important. Also, that I value myself enough to book the time and follow through in order to keep the promise to myself.

Action I will take:
Book 1.5 hours a week to go for a walk in the forest on my own (or go for coffee, or to the spa, etc.)

Support I will need:
Someone to take the kids so I can keep my commitment to myself.

Conversations I will need to have:
• Set a boundary for meetings—instead of 60 minutes with no breaks in between, make them 45 minutes with a 10 minute break. • Ask my partner to support me when I want to let go of this promise to myself. • Ask my partner how I can support her in booking time for herself as well.

Create your plan here: (add additional lines to create a blank form for a plan)[92]

The Belief about balance I will need to shift, plus the Benefit:

How I will reframe this belief:

Action I will take:

Support I will need:

Conversations I will need to have:

---

92   Gratitude to New Ventures West for my Integral Coaching program methodology and practices that inform the development of Action Worksheets throughout the book.

8. Review and reflect

Review your work-life balance Assessment and reflect on what it tells you.

Notice how it feels and what arises for you in terms of emotions or thoughts. Write down what your experience was like using the following space:

How I felt:

What I noticed about my thoughts:

What emotions arose during this exercise, if any:

What this experience was like for me:

What I am learning about myself as a result:

ACTION WORKSHEET – STEP #7 REFLECT ON THE AWAKENING AND IMPLICATIONS /FOR YOUR LEADERSHIP

Use the following action worksheet to understand the awakening that may be created when you completed the first six steps of the Authentic You™ Personal Planning System and renewed your personal clarity. Also reflect on the implications for your leadership.

Reflect on your what you've learned about your Authentic Self, values, purpose, leadership principles, life vision and work-life balance assessment. Next, complete the following questions:

1. What are you learning about your life and how you would like to live aligned with Authentic Self? What are you becoming awake to?

2. How important is what you are learning about yourself? How is it important to you?

3. What are you learning about your leadership and how you would like to bring your Authentic Self into your day-to-day activities?

4. What are the implications for your leadership? What will you focus on for the next 3 months? For the next 12 months?

5. What are two strengths that will support you as you move forward?

6. What are two self-limiting beliefs that it will be helpful to shift or let go of, in order for you to move forward? How can you reframe them to improve your leadership?

7. Is there any support you would need to have in order to be more authentic in your leadership?

8. Review and reflect

Read your responses to yourself. Notice how it feels and what arises for you in terms of emotions or thoughts. Write a statement that describes your awakening, and your understanding of the implications for your leadership and your life.

The awakening is:

The implications for my leadership are:

The implications for my life are:

Write down what your experience was like using the following space:

How I felt:

What I noticed about my thoughts:

What emotions arose during this exercise, if any:

What this experience was like for me:

What I am learning about myself as a result:

ACTION WORKSHEET – STEP #8
SET YOUR GOALS

Use the following action worksheet to develop your goals (personal and business):

Reflect on your what you've learned about your Authentic Self, values, purpose, leadership principles and life vision (including any business or other goals you would like to set) and complete the following exercise:

1. Choose a time horizon that feels right for your life (i.e. 6 months, one year).

The time horizon that feels right for me is: _____

2. Review the work-life balance Assessment you completed and decide on the two to three areas in which you would like to see something different (i.e. the three lowest ratings for where you are currently spending your energy compared to the optimal level. For the example above it is career, spirituality and health).

The parts of my life I would like to see change are:

a)

b)

c)

3. Set a goal or an intention for each of these parts of your life that will provide focus for your choices and actions for the next applicable timeframe. Make the goal as specific and clear as possible. Intentions are more general and set the tone and provide a theme for the next timeframe.

Examples of goals include:

- Career/Business—Increase gross sales to $5M annually by December.
- Personal Development—Find a community of support by September and attend 6 group sessions by December.
- Health—practice yoga 2-3 times per week for an hour—have a consistent practice by May.

Examples of intentions are:

- Career/business—to improve sales by cultivating exceptional customer experiences
- Personal development—find a community and practice accepting support
- Health—to create the conditions for a renewed sense of strength and wellness

1. Area of my life I would like to see change occur in:
Goal or intention:

2. Area of my life I would like to see change occur in:
Goal or intention:

3. Area of my life I would like to see change occur in:
Goal or intention:

Record these in your Authentic Leadership Authentic You™ Personal Learning Journal™ or on the poster (so you have all your information on one page).

4. Decide on one action that is the next step that you can take to achieve your goals—this can be for the next day, week, month, quarter, or however long you think you need to complete this step. Record these as well. Some examples are:

- Career/Business: Implement the social networking strategy in the next month (by June).
- Spirituality: Talk to 3 people whom I admire, and ask them how they include spirituality in their life (if they do) and where they find their community of support (by July).
- Health: Sign up for a monthly package at a yoga studio or download a free Yoga App on my SmartPhone (by April 15).

1. Goal or intention:
One action I will take to move forward:

2. Goal or intention:
One action I will take to move forward:

3. Goal or intention:
One action I will take to move forward:

5. Review and reflect

Review your goals and reflect on the implications for your life. Are they realistic? Achievable? At a level of difficulty that is within 10% of your comfort zone?

Notice how it feels and what arises for you in terms of emotions or thoughts. Write down what your experience was like using the following space:

How I felt:

What I noticed about my thoughts:

What emotions arose during this exercise, if any:

What this experience was like for me:

What I am learning about myself as a result:

6. Review your goals on a regular basis and reflect on whether they need to be adjusted or whether you have achieved them. Make adjustments where necessary.

Dates I will review my goals and/or intentions in order to keep them fresh and clear:

Date:

Date:

Date:

Date:

ACTION WORKSHEET – STEP #9
CREATE YOUR INNER DEVELOPMENT PLAN

Use the following action worksheet to create your inner development plan:

Creating a development plan for the inner development begins with an understanding of what goals you want to accomplish and an awareness of limiting beliefs and behaviours that might be getting in the way.

You may be able to complete all or part of your inner development plan on your own, and/or it may be helpful to work with a guide who can see potential blind spots. This could include your supervisor, a friend, a mentor, and/or a coach.

1. Begin by relaxing, centering and opening to these exercises.

2. Reflect on your what you've learned about your Authentic Self, values, purpose, leadership principles, life vision, work-life balance, goals, and answer the following question:
Given who I am at my best and what I want to accomplish, both at work and at home, are there any beliefs or behaviours that if I shifted them or let them go, would support me at this time?
Review the following example and, using your goals, identify limiting beliefs and/or behaviours below:

My goal:	Limiting belief or behaviour:
Learn how to delegate more effectively within 3 months.	Impatience with others who complete tasks differently than you would; judging other approaches—believing that using a different approach than yours will not produce as good a result.

Next, research what exercises you can do to achieve each goal and to create new behaviours that will support achieving it. In addition, identify exercises you can complete for awareness and self-management.

Use the following table of examples for ideas, and inner development plan form to complete your plan.

INNER DEVELOPMENT PLAN—IDEAS FOR EXERCISES

The following table shows several pages of sample goals within an organizational context (for situations that are frequently learning "edges" for leaders at one time or another in their career), as well as sample actions and exercises for your inner development plan.

Consider these exercises for your Authentic You™ Personal Planning System if you are having challenges in these areas. Note—for most examples in this table the timeframe is 3 months. This may vary depending on the amount of time required to actually achieve the internal shifts required and to create the new behaviours. As you begin to understand the length of time needed for yourself, you can adjust the time in your inner development plan.

Your goal:
Learn how to delegate more effectively within 3 months.
Limiting belief or behaviour and mindset shift required:
Impatience with others who complete tasks differently than you would have; judging other approaches—believing that using a different approach than yours will not produce as good a result.
Mindset shift required: To see delegation as essential to your effectiveness, and getting things done through others as efficient rather than an extra effort. Delegating also gives the other person the chance to shine!
Exercises to help shift or let go of it:
Each week create a list of 5 things that need to get done, who can complete them (not you), and what support you can provide so they learn. Assign the task and support the person as they complete it.
Exercises for awareness and self-managing:
Awareness – Pay attention to what happens for you (i.e. your anxiousness, lack of trust, and desire to take the work back and do it yourself) when the person completes the work differently from how you would have.
Self-managing - Practice self-managing and talk to the person with a non-judgmental tone in order to check understanding; provide feedback and ask them to make the changes themselves.

Your goal:
Improve your ability to give up resources when this is the right answer for the company—within 1 week.
Limiting belief or behaviour and mindset shift required:
Blaming peers in other departments for getting resources that you wanted to acquire for your own projects. Mindset shift required—Doing the right thing for the customer and company is essential. Use the company vision and values as a starting point for working together; collaboration between departments is the key.
Exercises to help shift or let go of it:
In your resource allocation meeting, practice giving up one thing that is low risk for your team.
Exercises for awareness and self-managing:
Awareness – Pay attention to the process—what occurs in your mind. The process of blaming may arise in this discussion. The content may be blaming because you believe the person doesn't value you and you judge yourself as weak if you give up any resources. Self-managing – Notice what happens for you internally when you give up the resource, and what the reaction is of the person you give it to. Reflect on the benefits for the team and the company. Debrief this experience with your supervisor and do one thing personally to celebrate your willingness to shift.

Your goal:
Be a more effective manager—within 3 months.

Limiting belief or behaviour and mindset shift required:
Getting defensive when people disagree with you or challenge your assumptions. Mindset shift required—Realizing you are doing something right to create a great environment in which people feel safe enough to share their opinions, particularly when they may cause disagreement. Thank them for challenging you.

Exercises to help shift or let go of it:
In 1:1 and group interactions, encourage team members to disagree with you and to challenge your assumptions in order to ensure that you have more complete information for decision making.

Exercises for awareness and self-managing:
Awareness - Pay attention to what happens in your body (thoughts, emotions) when others challenge you. Using *The Wisdom of the Enneagram* book, review the Levels of Development for your personality type,to understand what your healthy levels look like, and review the exercises suggested for when your type is under stress. Reflect on what your automatic pattern is. Self-managing – Practice deepening your breathing and staying open to hearing what other people have to say. Watch your tone and body language as you respond. Practice letting go of judgments as they arise and ask questions to clarify your understanding.

Your goal:
Improve your communication skills in difficult or uncomfortable situations—within 3 months.
Limiting belief or behaviour and mindset shift required:
Avoiding difficult conversations and/or being unaware of their impact on others.
Mindset shift required—Difficult conversations are opportunities to strengthen a relationship; they get less difficult with practice.
Exercises to help shift or let go of it:
Practice clearing issues within 24 hours of when they occur, so they don't become big issues.
Exercises for awareness and self-managing:
Awareness – Pay attention to your current pattern and how you think about clearing issues. (Do you avoid them at all cost? Do you get angry and defensive and show it in your tone and body language?
Self-managing - Practice using the arc of intense energy model to breathe and stay present through the conversation while you clear the issue.

Your goal:		
Improve your healthy debating skills in Leadership Team meetings on highly contentious strategic issues—within 3 months.		
Limiting belief or behaviour and mindset shift required:		
A fear of debating; seeing it as aggressive Mindset shift required—As an introvert, you can learn to enjoy debating as a kind of healthy sparring to come up with the best solution—just keep it focused on ideas rather than people.		
Exercises to help shift or let go of it:		
In each team meeting, prepare prior to the meeting and write down ideas for questions. Ask three questions and then state your opinion.		
Exercises for awareness and self-managing:		
Awareness - Notice what occurs for you in your body when you interact with team members. Notice your assumptions about their reactions and practice staying present through uncomfortable feelings that may arise. Self-managing - Practice deep breathing and relaxing as you continue to engage in the conversation. After the meeting reflect on one thing you did well and one thing you could have done differently. Incorporate these learnings in the next team meeting.		

Your goal:
Practice focus and discipline for more effective time management— within 3 months.
Limiting belief or behaviour and mindset shift required:
Avoiding planning; not thinking strategically.
Mindset shift required—Ongoing time to step back to see the forest, will allow you to be more effective when you go back into the day-to-day of walking amongst the trees.
Exercises to help shift or let go of it:
Using your Authentic You™ Personal Planning System (particularly your purpose and life vision) as context, once each quarter, practice prioritizing and planning for the next month, quarter and the balance of the year.
Exercises for awareness and self-managing:
Awareness - Pay attention to how you think about planning and whether you value it or not. If you do not value it, practice thinking about it in a different way—in a way that allows you to be enthusiastic about, it or at the least accept that planning will support you to be more effective. Before doing the planning exercise, reflect on how you can do it, and where, so that it aligns with your purpose and life vision (i.e. you can do it on a weekend away, or you can make your favorite meal as a celebration once it is complete). Reflect on how you currently plan, and how it would feel if it you did it in a way that is aligned with your authentic self.
Self-managing – When you are planning and you notice discomfort, practice self-managing to be aware of what is coming up for you. Reflect on what is behind the discomfort and what you are learning about yourself as a result.

My inner development plan:

Your goal:

Limiting belief or behaviour and mindset shift required:

Exercises to help shift or let go of it:

Exercises for awareness and self-managing:

Your goal:

Limiting belief or behaviour and mindset shift required:

Exercises to help shift or let go of it:

Exercises for awareness and self-managing:

Your goal:

Limiting belief or behaviour and mindset shift required:

Exercises to help shift or let go of it:

Exercises for awareness and self-managing:

Your goal:

Limiting belief or behaviour and mindset shift required:

Exercises to help shift or let go of it:

Exercises for awareness and self-managing:

5. Review and reflect

Review your inner development plan. Notice how it feels and what arises for you in terms of emotions or thoughts. Write down what your experience was like using the following space:

How I felt:

What I noticed about my thoughts:

What emotions arose during this exercise, if any:

What this experience was like for me:

What I am learning about myself as a result:

ACTION WORKSHEET
PUTTING IT INTO PRACTICE

Use the following action worksheet to put your Authentic You™ Personal Planning System into practice.

EXERCISES:

1. Decide on how often you will do a complete review your Authentic You™ Personal Planning System and Authentic You™ Personal Learning Journal. Will it be monthly, quarterly, annually?

Complete your review by re-doing each step. Make any changes to improve your Work-life balance, or set a different goal, as you become aware of a next self-limiting belief or behaviour, that would be helpful to shift.

2. Once you have completed the review, make adjustments in your Personal Learning Journal or create a new Authentic You™ Poster.

Reflect on how these changes feel. Notice what you are learning about yourself as you undertake this exercise and share your learnings with someone you trust and can be yourself with.

3. Another time to do a wholesale review is when you are at a crossroads in your life or career, or when a major life event has occurred. In addition, there may be a time when it simply feels right.

Review all the components of your Authentic You™ Personal Planning System and make adjustments where required. Notice how different possibilities for the future show up and how your choices and actions take on a new focus as a result.

4. Share the changes with others you feel comfortable with—family and friends, and members of your community of support.

COMMUNITY OF SUPPORT

Complete the following to create your community of support.

1. Reflect on who you have in your life who would be willing to support you on your journey to living as your Authentic Self. You may or may not have a community of support already in place. Write their names here:

2. Research communities of support that feel aligned to your values and life vision, and leadership principles. If you cannot find one, you may want to create one. List five people who might be interested in participating as a peer-mentoring group or community of support:

    1.

    2.

    3.

    4.

    5.

3. List your Personal Board of Directors or Dream team members as well as the kind of advice and guidance you seek them out for:

Who:	What guidance you see them out for:	When you will meet with them next:

Choose people with whom there is an alignment of values, with whom your energy builds when you are around them, who inspire you to be a better person and with whom you want to be in relationship for many years.

Notice how it is to be choiceful about whom you spend time with.

Reflect on what you are learning about yourself and write down your thoughts here:

APPENDIX B
ADDITIONAL MATERIAL

- Cultivating Authentic Leadership on Teams
- Hardwiring Authentic Leadership into your Organization
- Authenticity Checklist
- Interview with the Author

CULTIVATING AUTHENTIC LEADERSHIP ON TEAMS

The following are suggestions for cultivating Authentic Leadership on teams.

1. Share the following from Patrick Lencioni as context. He has a simple and useful model for describing five qualities of high-performing teams[93].

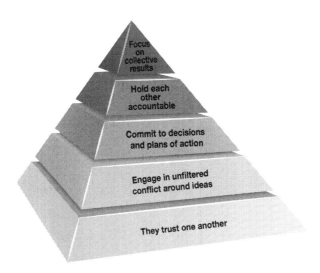

Source: Patrick Lencioni, "Five Dysfunctions of a Team"

The team will be as effective, as the collective capabilities of the individuals on the team.

Authentic leaders, who are the team members, support the healthy functioning of the team. They have the ability to model and behave in ways that build long-term, trust-based relationships.

In order for each of the team members to awaken their Authentic Leadership, use the following process:

---

93   Patrick Lencioni, Five Dysfunctions of a Team, p 189 – 190.

2. Each person reads this book and completes the Authentic You™ Personal Planning System. They gather in a ½ day retreat to share with the full team, what they are learning about themselves. This is a practice of showing appropriate vulnerability and empathy. Getting to know each other on a more personal level supports building a foundation of trust.

This is especially useful for a new team, or for a team of people who have worked together for a long time and have new members joining, or where they need to take the team to a new level of effectiveness.

3. Complete the team strategic planning once this personal clarity by individuals has been articulated and shared. The possibilities for the team may be different once each individual has reconnected to their Authentic Self.

4. Next have each person complete their personal objectives, as part of the performance development system. The personal clarity will inform these objectives, again with a refreshed lense to see different possibilities.

5. On an ongoing basis, gather the team to check in on their progress, understand what is challenging for them, and what they would like to share with others. Do this in the context of a seperate topic each time. This will act as a way of recharging the group as they continue their daily practice of the 4 steps to becoming an authentic leader – awakening, awareness, action, and deepening awareness.

6. Where team members are leaders of a department, they can then repeat this process with their department team as well.

HARDWIRING AUTHENTIC
LEADERSHIP INTO YOUR ORGANIZATION

The following are suggestions for hardwiring Authentic Leadership into your organization:

1. Model it – starting with the executives

While I have seen successful cultural change begin with mid-level teams, the most successful way to strengthen the culture begins with the leaders setting the direction and modeling the behaviours that are acceptable and expected.

Use the Authentic You™ Personal Planning System as a leadership development and team building exercise. Each of the executive review the book, and complete the Authentic You™ Personal Planning System action worksheets. They they come together as part of an annual retreat to share what they are learning about themselves.

Each executive requests feedback and receives it from the others on the team – particularly around self-limiting beliefs and how to reframe them, and practices for inner development. This personal clarity then informs the annual organizational strategic planning process.

2. Integrate it into your hiring practices and new hire orientation

Creating a culture of authenticity is supported by hiring people who are already on their personal journey to becoming authentic.

Use the four characteristics of an authentic leader in the interview process to request examples of behaviours that are consistent with authenticity – personal clarity, consistency in all parts of their life, choiceful behaviour based on this clarity and ethics, and caring – for themselves, for others and for the world.

Once the right people have been hired, include the Authentic You™ Personal Planning System as a part of the new-hire orientation program. In addition to supporting their effectiveness as a leader, this will also provide information for them personally and their supervisor, when planning their career path.

3. Embed it in your human resource processes and procedures

The Authentic You™ Personal Planning System is a natural addition to the performance development process in your organization. It can be completed and/or adjusted annually prior to setting personal objectives for the year. It will open up new possibilities for how to achieve stretch targets as leaders focus on their strengths and let go of self-limiting beliefs and behaviours. It will also support the development of emotional and social intelligence.

In addition, learning and development programs, can include facilitated workshops to support understanding of the right mindset and 4 steps to becoming an authentic leader. Ongoing support for individual development is done through, ongoing programs, community building and targetted 1:1 and group coaching.

Succession planning and retirement transition planning, can both be supported by individuals completing the Authentic You™ Personal Planning System prior to the mutual decision making required to make these transitions successful.

And finally, where people are not a right fit for an organization, completing the Authentic You™ Personal Planning System, after they leave an organization, can be an essential part of their healing process and ability to move forward. The personal learning that occurs when they accept responsibility for their part, and understand blindspots, can create an awakening and will be helpful for them to find the right fit for their career and life in the future as well.

4. Leverage technology to create community

It is essential to have one or more communities of support as leaders incorporate a daily practices of the 4 steps to becoming authentic – awakening, awareness, action and deepening awareness. By talking to others and hearing their stories, they will be recharged and recommitted to continuing their journey to becoming authentic.

Technology supports community building – both with live, facilitated Authenticity Recharges™, as well as videos, online interaction using Yammer, or Wikis, or equivalent software that supports team members providing peer-to-peer support. This also supports cross-company collaboration, as opposed to siloed competition.

5. Recognize and celebrate it

Whenever you experience Authentic Leadership, fan the flame and celebrate it. The more people are recognized, both formally, and informally, they more they will continue to learn.

AUTHENTICITY CHECKLIST

Use the following checklist to check your understanding and ability to live and lead authentically. Complete the self-reflection on page two and feel free to join the conversation on our facebook page.

Rate each of the following using a 5-point scale (1 – Strongly Disagree; 2 - Disagree; 3 – Not sure; 4 – Agree; 5 – Strongly Agree):

My understanding of Authenticity:
___ I understand what a leader is
___ I understand what an authentic person is
___ I understand how I am being a leader in my life
___ I understand the 4 Cs of authenticity
___ I understand the difference between authentic self and personality (or ego)
___ I understand what aspects of my personality that are supporting my effectiveness
___ I understand what aspects of my personality are limiting my effectiveness
___ I understand what the process is to become authentic (defined by the 4 As)

Personal Clarity:
___ I understand who I am as my authentic self (who I am when at my best)
___ I understand what my values are
___ I understand what higher purpose is (my gift or what I was intended to do)
___ I understand what my leadership principles are (how I want to translate my authentic self into tangible day-to-day leadership activities)
___ I understand what my life vision is
___ I understand what my current vs. optimal work-life balance is
___ I understand what my current awakening/wake-up call is and the

implications for my life
___ I understand what my goals are (personal)
___ I understand what my goals are (business/career)
___ I understand what the next step for my inner development plan is

Foundational Competencies for Authenticity:
___ I have foundational practices for wellness in place to support authenticity
___ I am aware of my boundaries and what is acceptable to me
___ I am able to say no, where no is what I mean
___ I am aware of the inner critic and unable to manage it
___ I am able to live with a feeling of balance between all parts of my life
___ I am able to have difficult conversations
___ I am able to manage conflict – to clear annoyances before they become big issues
___ I am able to live with awareness of the three centres of intelligence (thinking, emotions, sensing/intuition) and to integrate all of them into my day-to-day decision making

Self Reflection:

Reflect on your ratings and decide on 3 areas for development at this time.
Integrate these into your goals or intentions.
Revisit this checklist from time to time to determine any areas for development that could support you to live authentically.

1.

2.

3.

Record any questions you have about authenticity:

Record any other thoughts or learnings here:

INTERVIEW WITH THE AUTHOR

What inspired you to write this book?

There are a couple of reasons why I wanted to write this book – first it took me many years to finally find where I fit in the world and to feel settled with a sense of personal contentment and meaning.

In addition, I have a passion for business, as well as a for leadership and personal development that I wanted a way to pair and share with others. And finally, I wanted a way to do my part – to help in the world, and I love to support leaders within organizations.

I have seen many people struggle either with trying to be themselves when they have been told they need to be something different in order to succeed. Or when they are impacted and find it difficult to live their true potential as their supervisors create negative conditions, they lose confidence and aren't sure how to move forward.

Over the years I have had the support of others and it has lead me to the understandings and experiences that are found in the book. So I thought I'd share them with others in the hopes that it will help them find where they fit, find meaning in what they do, and cultivate a way of being that is supportive for themselves, their teams and the world at large.

What are the top 3 learnings you would like leaders to take away after reading it?

First, that you are whole and perfect as who you are right now.

Second, that you can have a life of meaning, and realize the business benefits through this.

Third, by understanding what inner development is, you can learn to manage it and have more choice in your decisions and external experiences.

And finally (I'll be choiceful and add an additional point) build and foster community as you enter this life-long practice.

ABOUT THE AUTHOR

Tana Heminsley is a thought leader, author, and facilitator in the area of Authentic Leadership and Emotional Intelligence.

She is an executive and an entrepreneur with a passion for building businesses and developing leaders.

In 1984, at 22, Tana was national correspondent for CP Rail's in-house newsletter for the $600-million Roger's Pass tunnel project; at 27, she opened Tana Lee, a retail clothing store in Revelstoke, B.C. She's worked for the founders of the balanced scorecard management system, which originated out of Harvard and she's consulted on strategy implementation around the US.

She has been a member of the Executive team for BC Hydro – one of North America's leading providers of clean, renewable energy - with 4,500 employees, annual net income of $400 Million (2007) and 1.7 million customers. Tana was Director, Stakeholder Engagement where she was accountable for involving the public in dialogue with BC Hydro regarding a number of topics including long-term energy planning.

Tana holds an MBA from Simon Fraser University, Vancouver, B.C. Canada.

She is an Executive and Leadership Coach, (member of the International Coaching Federation; and an Integral Coach trained through New Ventures West). She is also a Certified Professional EQ Analyst, is a Certified Authentic Leadership Program Facilitator. She has completed the Enneagram Intensive training and is a member of the Professional Enneagram Association of Canada (PEAC).

Tana is a Business Mentor and Executive Coach with ViRTUS Inc. – a Vancouver-based organization focused on strategy, leadership, team building – all with a foundation of authentic leadership, emotional and social intelligence. She works as part of a team for the delivery of a 40,000 person global training program for the implementation of a Emotional and Social Intelligence program. Delivery of the program is being done both face-to-face, as well as virtually using Avatars and Web.Alive.

She is also the founder of Authentic Leadership Global, Inc. – a growing global community.

Made in the USA
Charleston, SC
22 June 2013